Library Celebrations

Cindy Dingwall

Alleyside Press®

Fort Atkinson, Wisconsin

Acknowledgements

Many thanks to:

All of the libraries I used during the creation of this book. They include: Arlington Heights Memorial Library, Barrington Area Library, Ela Area Library, Mount Prospect Public Library, Palatine Area Library, Prospect Heights Public Library, Schaumburg Public Library District and Vernon Area Library.

The members of Lincoln Story League for providing authors, librarians and storytellers with a safe place to share and try out new ideas.

Published by **Alleyside Press**, an imprint of Highsmith Press
Highsmith Press
W5527 Highway 106
P.O. Box 800
Fort Atkinson, Wisconsin 53538-0800
1-800-558-2110

© Cindy Dingwall, 1999
Cover design: Frank Neu

The paper used in this publication meets the minimum requirements of American National Standard for Information Science — Permanence of Paper for Printed Library Material. ANSI/NISO Z39.48-1992.

Library of Congress Cataloging-in-Publication Data
  Dingwall, Cindy
    Library celebrations / Cindy Dingwall.
      p. cm.
    Includes bibliographical references.
    ISBN 1-57950-027-7 (pbk. : alk. paper)
    1. Children's libraries--Activity programs--United States.
    2. Puzzles.   I. Title.
  Z718.2.U6D56   1999
  027.62 ' 5--dc21   98-50401
                        CIP

Contents

To my friend Carolyn Reinhard,
who shares my love of libraries,
books and reading.

Introduction

Library Celebrations is about celebrating all of the great things your library has to offer, and helping you to spread the word throughout your community about the diverse and exciting things you have going on. Today's libraries are bustling with activities and programming that promote learning as well as recreational reading, listening, connecting and viewing.

There are six full programs here that highlight your library or important celebrations about books and reading. Each program features storytelling, music, games, activities, crafts and of course refreshments. A Reading Program is suggested for each celebration. Also included are service projects that will benefit the library and its community.

These programs are intended for children aged three years through fifth grade. You can adapt them to meet the ages and needs of the group you are working with. Choose stories that are appropriate for the age group you are working with. To find additional stories about libraries and books and reading, look up these subjects in the catalog: Books and reading; Libraries; and Libraries--Fiction. Perform word searches for: book, books, reading, read, libraries, and library.

There is a large section of Library Puzzles. You can use these with any of the library celebrations you would like. Some of the puzzles reward children by offering stickers or stamps for correctly completed puzzles. Others encourage children to develop the library habit by including the check out of library materials as part of the activity. Try to offer a different puzzle at each event you host. For week-long celebrations such as Children's Book Week and National Library Week each child will have a booklet of puzzles if they collect a puzzle each day.

You may wish to create additional puzzles that highlight your library. For Children's Book Week and National Library Week, design puzzles that highlight this year's theme. Try to have one for each day of the week, so children have something new to look forward to each day.

Go now, and …

Celebrate Your Library!

Happy Birthday to Our Library

Find out when your town's library was founded. Celebrate the library's 25th, 50th, 75th, and 100th birthdays. You can adapt it for a school library if desired.

Program (60–90 minutes)

Welcome
Ask your board president (or another board member) to provide a brief welcome.

Story
The Story of Our Library: Invite a creative staff member to write a history of your library. Illustrate it with photographs, slides, samples of the kinds of books you had and other historic items. Have your library director or school librarian share this with the children.

Story
Choose any library story to share. (See page 8 for suggestions.)

Project
Design a Bookmark: Instructions on page 9.

Booktalks
Choose books that are about libraries and tell about them. Avoid telling how the stories end. Encourage the children to check out the books and read them to see how they end.

Who Is It?
Have six people (three men and three women) dress as famous Americans. Let them wander around the library. They can tell people how reading helped them (Abraham Lincoln; Helen Keller; Ben Franklin, making sure he tells children that he started the first lending library).

Activity
Library Treasure Hunt: Instructions on page 9–10.

Story
Choose any library story to share. (See page 8 for suggestions.)

Time Capsule
Purchase a large disaster-proof container. Fill the container with items from your library. Include photos of the library as it looks now. Also include: a library card, an overdue notice, pictures of the staff, photos of this year's celebration, a copy of the celebration program, a library newsletter, a list of favorite books, front page of today's newspaper, any press releases about your celebration and other things the children think of. Place this time capsule in a safe place. Open it on your next "big" birthday celebration.

Snacks
Have the children remain seated in the program area. Light the candles on the cake and sing "Happy Birthday" to the library. Bring each child a piece of cake and a cup of juice.

Conclusion
Cheer the Library: Instructions on pages 11–12.

 Ideas

Use birthday paper and ribbon to gift wrap the books you plan to use. Unwrap them to see the "surprise birthday book" as you prepare to share the story, or

Place all of the books you plan to share in a large box and gift wrap it. Unwrap the box and share each book with the children.

Planning and Promotion

Advertising Display

Have a birthday cake-shaped poster with numeral candles that indicate how old your library is. Print: CELEBRATE _____ LIBRARY'S ___ BIRTHDAY on the cake. Include program and registration information on the poster. Provide birthday-cake-shaped flyers with program and registration information for people to take as reminders.

Book Display

Have a display of fiction and informative books about libraries for children to check out.

Room Decorations

Try to find decorations that highlight birthdays, books and reading.

Snacks

Have a large cake shaped like a book. Print HAPPY BIRTHDAY _____ LIBRARY across the middle. Use numeral candles to indicate the library's age. Serve fruit punch as a beverage.

Special Guests

Try to locate and invite all former staff members to your birthday celebration. Ask each person to send birthday greetings to the library. Display these during your celebration. Then add them to your scrapbook. Set up a "reunion area" for former staff members to gather and visit with one another.

Camera and Film

Have a camera loaded with film. Take photos of the program to display later. Put some of them into the time capsule. (See page 7.)

Name Tags

Choose any self-stick birthday name tags.

Party Prize (Optional)

Give each guest a pencil with the library's name, address and phone number printed on it.

Preliminary Activities

Look in an atlas to find libraries in towns from other states that have the same name or one similar to your town's name. Write to them telling about your birthday celebration and ask them to respond by sending birthday greetings. Try to become "Library Pen Pals" with them. If you cannot find a town with the same or a similar name, choose a town in a city or town that is comparable to yours in size. You can try to receive birthday greetings from every state. *(This is a good Internet activity.)*

Program Resources

Caseley, Judith. *Sophie and Sammy's Library Sleepover.* Greenwillow Books, 1993. Sophie decides to have a library sleepover with her brother Sammy.

Clifford, Eth. *Help! I'm a Prisoner in the Library.* Houghton Mifflin, 1979. Imagine being accidentally locked in the library overnight. You might have some exciting adventures.

Deedy, Carmen Agra. *The Library Dragon.* Peachtree Press, 1994. The Library Dragon refuses to let anyone read the library books!

Houghton, Eric. *Walter's Magic Wand.* Orchard Books, 1990. Walter causes quite a commotion in the library. He has a magic wand that can bring stories to life.

Huff, Barbara. *Once Inside the Library.* Little, Brown, 1990. There are lots and lots of wonderful books to read once you get inside the library.

Kimmel, Eric. *I Took My Frog to the Library.* Viking Penguin, 1990. A little girl takes her pets to the library. What trouble they cause!

Landon, Lucinda. *Meg Mackintosh and the Mystery in the Locked Library.* Joy Street Press, 1993. A rare book has been stolen from the library. Can Meg and her friends find it?

Instructions for Design a Bookmark

Materials

- 1 colored piece of felt per child (8" x 2")
- glue (one small bottle per child)
- one envelope per child
- glitter and sequins
- fabric markers

Directions

1. Give each child the materials and let them design a bookmark.
2. Put each bookmark into an envelope labeled with the child's name. Seal it shut. Kids can take these home.

Instructions for Library Treasure Hunt

Each child will follow a color coded trail. Provide at least ten different paths for the children to follow. This keeps one area from becoming too congested. Alert the Circulation Desk to expect an influx of children checking out materials at the end of the hunt. Print each clue on a 5"x3" colored sheet of paper. The paper color for Clue 1 indicates the color path each treasure hunter should follow. Try this format.

Pre-School–Kindergarten: Red or blue (Have them hunt with the adult who brings them to the program.)

Grade 1: Purple or green (May need adult assistance.)

Grade 2: Yellow or orange (May need adult assistance.)

Grade 3: Pink or white

Grade 4: Beige or navy blue

Grade 5: Brown or lavender

Materials

- 1 large paper grocery bag per child *(Print each child's first and last name on their bag.)*
- clues
- black markers
- library cards *(Ask children to bring these to the program Collect them as they arrive and give them to the Circulation Desk. The cards will then be available for use during the Treasure Hunt. Return the cards to the children as they leave the program.)*

Additional Help

- volunteers to assist children on the hunt

Directions

Give each child Clue 1. The child must decipher that clue to find their next clue.

At that location, they will find Clue 2. They keep deciphering the clues until they arrive at each destination. If they ask where they go next say, "The clues will give you that information. Every clue you receive will tell you where to go next."

Hints

Have the volunteers serve as "Trail Blazers." Tell the children that the Trail Blazers are there to help them if they get stuck. However, remind the Trail Blazers to assist by encouraging the children to figure things out on their own. This includes having kids do their own keying for computer searches.

Have adults who brought preschoolers and kindergartners accompany them on the hunt. In schools, teachers and room parents can help. First and second graders may need extra help as well.

Sample Treasure Hunt (Grades 4–5)

Clue 1

Unscramble this book character's name.

SMR. GIPGLE ELGGIW

Look up this name in the catalog. Find out the author of these books. Go to that shelf and select one of the books about this character. Put the book in your bag. Look for a red piece of paper with *Clue 2* written on it.

Clue 2

Complete these math problems to find your next treasure and clue.

$$5 \quad 5 \quad 4 \quad 4$$
$$-2 \quad +4 \quad +4 \quad -2$$

Choose a book from these shelves. Put it in your bag. Look for a red piece of paper with *Clue 3* written on it.

Clue 3

Stop, Look and Listen! Where would you go to do that in this department?

Look for the red star. Take one of these items, and put it into your bag. Look for a red piece of paper with *Clue 4* written on it.

Clue 4

Twinkle, twinkle little ___ ___ ___ ___ S. What is the missing word? Print it here and look it up in the catalog. Write down the call number. Go to the shelves to find a book about this. Choose a book, put it in your bag and look for a red piece of paper with *Clue 5* printed on it.

Clue 5

These usually come out once a month. You might have a subscription to one of them. What are they? Go to that area and choose one to take home. Put it in your bag. Look for a red piece of paper with *Clue 6* written on it.

Clue 6

This is the place where you check out books. Go there and check out the materials in your bag. Look for a red piece of paper with *Clue 7* written on it.

Clue 7

Return to the program room for more fun and snacks!

Hints

Label each child's bag with their first and last name.

Have Circulation Staff return the library cards to you. Give children cards and bags at the end of the program.

Answers to the Treasure Hunt

1. Mrs. Piggle Wiggle by Betty MacDonald. 2. 398.2 (Fairy Tale Shelf). 3. Audiovisual Area (The star will be by the audiocassettes). 4. Stars 523.8. 5. Magazine section. 6. Circulation Desk. 7. Program Room.

Suggestions

- Use registration information to make up age-appropriate hunts. For example, a first grader can be given cards with pictures (storybook, informative book, or magazine) on them. Cards with matching pictures can be at each location.

- Clues for preschool and kindergarten children may include: Look for a star (nonfiction books). Choose a book from that shelf. Look for a triangle (audiocassettes). Choose an audiocassette.

- Clues for first, second and third grades may include: Look on the fiction shelf for the letters A–B. Choose a book from that shelf and put it into your bag. Look for a book by (author's name) and put it in your bag. Look for a fairy tale (398.2) and choose a book to put in your bag. Look for a magazine to put in your bag. Go to the audiovisual section. Choose a book and cassette packet to put in your bag. You can also use picture clues.

- Have books and topics that interest both boys and girls.

- Remind children, "This is not a race to see who finishes first. *Everyone* will finish and *everyone* will win."

- If children ask about prizes say, "Your prizes are in your bags."

- The final clue will lead them to the circulation desk where they will check out the materials in their bags. Give the cards and bags to the children (or adult who brought them) as they leave the program. Remind them to take them home to enjoy and bring them back by the due date marked on them. Be sure to explain this to the adults who bring the children to the program.

Instructions for Cheer the Library

Cheer is on page 12.

Materials

- 7 pieces of white poster board (12" x 12")
- bright, colorful markers (*red, green, blue, red, purple work best*)
- laminating film and machine or clear contact paper

Additional Help

- 7 kids to hold the letters that spell LIBRARY

Preparation

1. Write one letter on one side of each piece of poster board, so that the word LIBRARY is spelled out. Use large, capital letters.

2. Laminate each card (or cover with clear contact paper).

Directions

1. Choose seven children to help. Each child holds one letter. They stand facing the audience, so that the letters of the word library will appear in the proper order.

2. Have them hold the cards in front of them, face down, so the letters cannot be seen. Make sure when they flip the cards up, the letters appear right-side up.

Additional Activities: Birthday Presents for the Library

A Penny a Day

Years ago, library fines used to be "a penny a day." Place a large, glass jar on the circulation counter. Ask patrons to put their pennies into the jar. Count these on a monthly basis, and deposit them into a special account. Keep a running total of the pennies collected. Post that information on a monthly basis. At the end of the year, use the pennies to purchase something special for the children's department.

Birthday Cards

Borrow an old, no longer used postal box from the neighborhood post office. Provide colored paper, crayons, pencils (regular and colored). Invite children to design a birthday card for the library. They can mail it in the mailbox. Empty the box and display the cards in a visible location.

Birthday Books Club

Begin a "Birthday Books Club" in your library. During the month of their birthday, children can select a book from one of your new books. Parents donate the cost of the selected book and their child's name is printed on a specially designed bookplate. Add the bookplate to the book and let the child be the first to check it out. Take a photo of each child holding their donated book. Create an eye-catching "Birthday Books Club" display with photos and names of children who are members. Publicize this program in your newsletter and the local newspaper.

Cheer the Library!

LEADER:	Give us an L *(child holds card over head)*
AUDIENCE:	*L*
LEADER:	Give us an I *(child holds card over head)*
AUDIENCE:	*I*
LEADER:	Give us B *(child holds card over head)*
AUDIENCE:	*B*
LEADER:	Give us an R *(child holds card over head)*
AUDIENCE:	*R*
LEADER:	Give us an A *(child holds card over head)*
AUDIENCE:	*A*
LEADER:	Give us an R *(child holds card over head)*
AUDIENCE:	*R*
LEADER:	Give us a Y *(child holds card over head)*
AUDIENCE:	*Y* *(Have kids return cards to down-in-front position.)*
LEADER:	What does it spell? *(kids hold cards over heads)*
AUDIENCE:	*LIBRARY! (cards down)*
LEADER:	Where can we go to find good books? *(cards up)*
AUDIENCE:	*LIBRARY! (cards down)*
LEADER:	Where can we go to find cassettes? *(cards up)*
AUDIENCE:	*LIBRARY! (cards down)*
LEADER:	Where can you go to find the answers? *(cards up)*
AUDIENCE:	*LIBRARY! (cards down)*
LEADER:	Where can we go to find a video? *(cards up)*
AUDIENCE:	*LIBRARY! (cards down)*
LEADER:	Where can we go to find magazines? *(cards up)*
AUDIENCE:	*LIBRARY! (cards down)*
LEADER:	Where can we go for great programs? *(cards up)*
AUDIENCE:	*LIBRARY! (cards down)*

REPEAT "GIVE US AN L" SEQUENCE

LEADER:	What do we love? *(cards up)*
AUDIENCE:	*OUR LIBRARY! (cards down)*
LEADER:	Let's say it loud and clear! We love our library! *(cards up)*
AUDIENCE:	*WE LOVE OUR LIBRARY!* *(cards down)*
LEADER:	Say it one more time! *(cards up)*
AUDIENCE:	*WE LOVE OUR LIBRARY!*
LEADER:	We love our library!
AUDIENCE:	*WE LOVE OUR LIBRARY! YEAH! YEAH1 YEAH!*

Hints

Have two signals. One to tell the children to raise cards, the other to lower them.

Have the "card holders" jump up as they display their cards.

Ideas

Ask a child to assume the role of "leader."

Have the children design and color the cards.

How Many Books?

Create a registration card that includes name, address, phone, school, grade, age and library card number for each child who participates. This allows you to compile useful statistical information. Whenever a child reads a book, let them fill out a book-shaped form (sample forms below).

Create a display on a large wall. As children turn in their forms "put their books on the shelves." See how many "shelves" of books the children can read.

Keep a running total of the books read. Will it exceed the number of children's books your library owns? Try to find a group that presents puppet shows based on children's stories to present a program for the children who participate. An alternative is to have staff members present a puppet show.

Registration Form

Registration Form for "How Many Books?"

Child's Name: _____

Address: _____

_____

Phone: _____ Age: _____ Grade: _____

School: _____ Library Card No: _____

Report Form

Title: _____

Author: _____

Your Name: _____

Summary: _____

_____

_____

_____

_____

Use 4"x 6" cards for each form.

Run the registration form on white cards.

Use a variety of colors for the report forms.

Welcome to Your New Library

This program is for the opening of a new building or the completion of a library addition or renovation.

Program (60–90 minutes)

Welcome
Ask the library board president to present a brief welcome.

Story
Building a Library: Invite a creative volunteer or staff member to tell the real story behind "Building the _____ Library." Be sure to encourage the writer to include some humorous events. Ask your director to share this at the program.

Project
Design a Bookmark: Instructions are on page 16.

Song
Our Library: Have someone write an original song about your library. It can have original music and lyrics or it can have lyrics set to a familiar tune that is in the public domain. Most important is that it be about your library. You might want to consider singing it at other library celebrations as well.

Story
Choose a story to share about building or beginning a library. See page 16 for suggestions.

Event
Library Quilt Dedication: Dedicate the quilt created by the children who participated in the "Quilt Making Program" detailed on page 17. If possible have the children who created the quilt squares and the quilters come up front for the dedication.

Where Is It Now?
Instructions are on page 16.

Booktalks
Choose several books about libraries to highlight. The more books you can find about building new libraries or starting libraries the better. Tell the story up to the climax, however avoid revealing the ending. Encourage listeners to find out how the story is resolved for themselves. There are suggestions on page 16.

Look Who's Visiting
Invite people to dress as characters from the books on building and starting new libraries. Let them tell your guests in their own words what it was like to be involved in the construction of a new library building.

Project
Passport to Your Library: Instructions on page 19.

Story
Choose any library story to share (page 16).

Snacks
Invite your guests to share in refreshments.

Conclusion
Cheer the Library: See pages 11–12 for instructions. Adapt the cheer to fit your new library.

Library Activity Book
Give each child their Library Activity Book to take home and use. See Party Prize on page 15 for ideas.

Advertising Display

Create a poster that has the architect's drawing of what your newly completed building will look like. Include photos of past and present buildings as well. Print the program and registration information on the poster. You can also include hammers and other construction materials. Design flyers that people can take as reminders.

Book Display

Have a display of books about libraries, especially books that are about building new libraries.

Room Decorations

Decorate the program room or area for a party. Try to find decorations (balloons, bunting, tablecloth, plates, cups, napkins) that highlight books, reading, audiovisual items, and computers. Design colorful banners to hang at the entrance to each department. These can be vertical banners with the name of the department printed vertically. You might want to make these banners permanent.

Snacks

Serve cake with the word Welcome written across it. Decorate it with library-related items (CDs, books, audiocassettes, etc.).

Name Tags

Choose any self-stick name tag that relates to books and reading.

Special Guests

Invite the mayor, superintendent of schools, school principals, school librarians, teachers, former staff members and other prominent citizens to share your festivities.

Camera and Film

Have a camera loaded with color film. Take photos of the ceremony and other activities. Purchase a large album, and begin a scrapbook about your library or the children's department. Include photos, newspaper articles and other information about your building project. This can become an ongoing project. Some photos can be put into the time capsule (see page 18).

Party Prize

Library Activity Books Give each child who attends a *Library Activity Book*. This will include puzzles and pictures to color. See pages 53–85 for puzzles that can be used. Design additional puzzles that are about your library and the services you offer. Try to include a drawing of your library that can be colored in. You might have pictures of the outside of your library, the children's room, and a group of kids reading.

Preliminary Activities

Your library already has a name, but does each department or meeting room have a name? Consider honoring special people (town founder, first children's librarian, etc.) by naming a department or meeting room after them.

Another idea is to have a "Naming Contest." Two months prior to your library opening, ask patrons to submit their ideas. Have a committee comprised of one person from each library department make the final decisions. Have attractive signs or banners made to hang outside the entrance to each department or meeting room. Make sure these are easy to read from a distance. Announce the names at New Library program.

Or if you have crafters, you might want to make a library quilt for permanent display. See page 17 for directions on making a quilt that you can unveil at the opening ceremony.

Program Resources

Alexander, Martha G. *How My Library Grew.* H.W. Wilson, 1983. A new library is being built across from Diana's house. How exciting to watch it grow.

Bauer, Caroline Feller. *Too Many Books.* Franklin Watts, 1984. Maralou has so many books that there isn't room for anyone or anything else in the house.

Cleary, Beverly. *Emily's Runaway Imagination.* William Morrow, 1961. Emily's mother is trying to organize the town's first library.

Greenwald, Sheila. *The Mariah Delany Lending Library Disaster.* Houghton Mifflin, 1977. Mariah decides to start her own lending library using her family's books. What a disaster!

Johnson, Jean. *Librarians A to Z.* Walter, 1988. Take an alphabetical tour of the library, and learn all of the interesting things that go on there.

Knowlton, Jack. *Books and Libraries.* HarperCollins, 1991. This book tells how books began and libraries were developed.

Stewart, Sarah. *The Library.* Farrar, Strauss, & Giroux, 1995. Elizabeth Browne had so many books that she decides to start a town library.

Materials and Prep

Instructions for Design a Bookmark

Materials

- one 11½"x 4" piece of white card stock per child
- crayons and markers
- clear contact paper

Directions

1. Give each child a piece of card stock.
2. Tell the children to use the crayons and markers to design a bookmark. Encourage them to decorate both sides.
3. Have each child write their name on the bookmark.
4. Cover bookmarks with clear contact paper and send them home with the children.

Instructions for Where Is It Now?

Materials

- 1 map of the children's department per child *(without labels or key)*
- 1 pencil per child
- 1 library/books/reading-related sticker per child

Additional Help

- someone to portray the "Map Maker"

Directions

1. Give each child a map and a pencil.
2. Tell the children that the "library map maker" drew the maps, but forgot to add the labels.
3. Ask the children to walk around the department, find out where things are, and print this on their maps.
4. Put a sticker on correctly labeled maps.
5. Just before children do Passport to Your Library have the Map Maker return with new maps that are correctly labeled due to children's help.

> **Hints**
>
> *Have staff members or volunteers on hand to help.*
>
> *Put signs indicating where things are at child height in addition to overhead signs.*
>
> *Make maps simple to label. Have a blank line drawn in each area you wish identified.*
>
> *Let them label areas such as picture books, beginning readers, biographies, nonfiction, fiction, holiday books, audiovisual, magazines, reference desk, program room.*

Materials and Prep

Instructions for Library Quilt

Have this program for children at least a month before the date of the Opening Ceremony. This gives you time to have the squares pieced and quilted so it will be ready to dedicate on the day of the program. Let everyone know it will be on permanent display.

Materials

- one 12"x 12"-square of drawing paper per child
- one white muslin 12"x 12"-square per child
- fabric markers and crayons
- pencils
- black marker
- book on quilting
- sewing machine, thread, needles
- quilt backing (*The size will depend upon how many quilt squares you have.*)

Additional Help

- Someone who is good at sewing. Quilting experience is very desirable.

Prior to the Program

On each square: Draw lines ¼" in from the sides to indicate to children that they should not draw beyond these lines. This is the seam allowance needed to join the pieces together.

Hints

Younger children will probably need the assistance of a parent.

Remind children to create original designs, not copies of pictures that are in the books they choose.

You may want to "suggest" books or stories to be used.

Be sure to include a picture and information about the quilt in your library newsletter, area newspapers and your Time Capsule.

Directions

1. Give each child a piece of drawing paper. Ask them to draw a picture from their favorite children's book or story. Feel free to set standards and limitations on the books and stories used.

2. When drawings are complete, outline the pictures in black marker.

3. Give each child a muslin square and tell them to lay it on top of their drawing.

4. Have them use pencils to trace the picture onto the muslin. Let them color the picture with fabric markers and crayons.

5. Make sure each child autographs their square.

6. Let these dry.

7. Have someone who is familiar with sewing and quilting make the squares into a quilt. Hanging handles will need to be added so that the quilt can be hung on permanent display.

8. Before the children leave, take a picture of them together. Be sure to write down their names in the order they are standing. Enlarge and frame the photo to hang on the wall next to the quilt. On a separate card list the children's names in an easy-to-read, bold-faced font. Frame this, and hang it and the photo next to the quilt.

Build a Library

Begin this several months before the opening of your new library. Draw a large outline of the outside of your library on pieces of large white butcher paper. Be sure to add windows and doors. Make it as realistic as possible. You will need to piece these together, so that it resembles what the outside of the finished building will look like. Make bricks in the same color as the exterior walls. Children can fill out one brick per book read. As children turn in their bricks, add them to the library. If you need more space, draw an outline of a second exterior wall of the library. See which building can be completed first. Adapt the registration form on page 13.

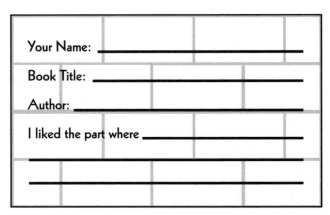

Brick Pattern

Within the brick:

Your Name: _____

Book Title: _____

Author: _____

I liked the part where _____

Additional Activities

Come On Over

Create an ongoing series of monthly programs for home daycare providers and their children and for homeschooling families. Include storytimes, booktalks, library skills programs, etc. Ask these groups how the library can better serve them.

Everything's Just Fine

During the first year in your new building, put peoples fines into a separate account. Keep a running total of the "Library Fines Collected To Date." At the end of the year, use the money to purchase something special for the Children's Department. Be sure to publicize what you used this money for.

Working at the Library

Invite present and former staff members to write a page about an interesting or amusing incident they remember happening while they were working at the library. Put these into a notebook and keep it on display for others to enjoy. Keep this as an ongoing activity. Years and years from now, future librarians can enjoy reading something about the "history" of the library.

Library Time Capsule

Purchase a large disaster proof container to make your Library Time Capsule. Copies of a current newspaper, your library newsletter, the Library Passport, the *Library Activity Book,* the program for your new library, along with photos (labeled) of staff and patrons, and any other items you choose should all go into your capsule. Put the capsule in a safe place until your library celebrates a milestone birthday. See pages 7–13.

Instructions for Passport to Your Library

Design a Library Passport. Give one to each child who attends the program. Have one page for each department visited. As children visit library departments, they will receive passport stamps. Each page can highlight department resources and activities. These can be highlighted for children on brief department tours. Departments can include: Children's Services, Young Adult, Adult, Audio-Visual, Periodicals, Technical Services, Circulation, Maintenance, etc.

You might include the names of the department coordinator and staff members who work in each area.

Children who visit all departments and show you a passport bearing stamps can be given a special prize or be invited to a special video or film presentation. This should be an enjoyable story about books, reading and/or libraries.

Sample Cover

Freetown Public Library

PASSPORT

Add your library's name to the front cover. Add graphics if you desire. Run the cover on a brightly colored piece of 8½" x 11" card stock.

Interior Page

CHILDREN'S DEPARTMENT

The children's department is filled with books, music cassettes and CD's, books on tape, book/cassette packets, videos, magazines, puzzles and more. We have many special programs for children. Stop by the Children's Reference Desk to say hello and ask for help.

Make a similar page for each department in your library. Run the passport pages on white paper. Fold the cover and pages in half to make a booklet. Put three staples down the crease.

Celebrate National Library Week

National Library Week (NLW) occurs in April. Check with the American Library Association for the exact dates and the annual theme. Order your materials as early as possible, so that they are on hand well before NLW.

Kick-Off Program for National Library Week (60–90 minutes)

You can do this on the Sunday or Monday that begins National Library Week.

Welcome

Invite the president of the library board or school board to present a brief welcome.

Story

Select a story that highlights this year's NLW theme. Read or tell it to the children.

Story

All About Libraries: Have a creative staff member or volunteer write a brief history of libraries. Begin with Ben Franklin, who created the first lending library. Include something about the changing and expanding nature of libraries from quiet reading rooms to lively community information centers. If desired, you can create a brief slide or sound show about your library and all it has to offer to share with your audience.

Game

Tour the Library: Instructions are on page 23.

Song

Oh, How We Love the Library: Song is on page 22.

Booktalks

Select books and other materials that highlight the NLW theme. Present short booktalks on these. Tell the story up to the climax, but don't reveal the ending. Encourage children to check these out to enjoy at home where they can see how they end. You can also highlight some of the books from the resource list on page 21.

Project

Book Posters: Instructions are on page 22.

Story

Select a story that highlights this year's theme. Present this story in a creative way, such as a puppet show, creative dramatics, etc.

Bookmarks

Instructions are on page 22.

Conclusion

Read Books Cheer: Instructions are on pages 32–33. If desired, adapt this to highlight the NLW theme.

Snacks

Bring each person a piece of cake and a cup of juice.

Planning and Promotion

Advertising Display

Use the posters and other promotional materials from the American Library Association (ALA) to create an eye-catching display inviting people to celebrate National Library Week. See page 88 for ALA's address.

Materials Display

Set up a display of library materials that highlights libraries and reading. Encourage people to check these out. You can also include materials that highlight this year's theme.

Room Decorations

Decorate the room to represent this year's theme. Use bunting, banners, posters and balloons. Use paper goods that highlight the theme or books and reading.

Name Tags

Find self-stick name tags that represent this year's theme. You can create your own using shapes from flannelboard pattern or clip art books. Stickers can be applied to self-stick name tags.

Snacks

Decorate a cake to highlight this year's theme. Have fruit juice for the beverage.

Special Guests

Invite your library board members to be an active part of your celebration. Other guests can include the town mayor and other officials, local authors, school principals and teachers.

Camera and Film

Have a camera loaded with color film. Take photos of the program. Display them for others to enjoy before adding them to your library scrapbook. (See Camera and Film on page 15 for directions on starting a scrapbook.)

Party Prizes

Give each child a large map of the library. These will be used for Tour the Library, found on page 23.

Preliminary Activities

Several weeks prior to NLW, send letters to school principals, day care and preschool directors and all teachers asking them to list their favorite children's books. Ask them to include a photo of themselves as well. Display the photos and letters on a wall so patrons can enjoy them. (A sample letter is on page 90. Adapt it as needed.) At the end of the week, purchase a large scrapbook and put the letters and photos into it. Keep it on permanent display in the children's department.

Program Resources

Brillhart, Julie. *Story Hour, Starring Megan.* Whitman, 1992. When Megan's mother is too busy to do storytime, Megan takes over with amazing results.

Brookfield, Karen. *Book.* Knopf, 1993. This book tells about the development of written languages and books.

Conford, Ellen. *Jenny Archer, Author.* Little, Brown, 1989. Jenny is supposed to write her autobiography, but she feels her life is dull. So, she embellishes her life story, just a bit.

Fritz, Jean. *The Man Who Loved Books.* Putnam, 1981.

Columba loves books, but he has trouble finding any to read.

Good Books. Good Times. Harper & Row, 1990. This book is overflowing with poems about books and reading.

Heller, Nicholas. *A Book for Woody.* Greenwillow Books, 1995. The books in Grandpa's house want Woody to read them.

Instructions for Book Posters

Materials

- one 11"x14" piece of white construction paper per child *(practice sheet is optional)*

- one 11"x14" piece of poster board per child *(optional)*

- crayons, markers, pencils *(glitter and glue are optional)*

Directions

1. Give each child a piece of paper.

2. Tell them to design a poster that encourages children to read books. Have each child autograph their poster. *(In public libraries, print the child's phone number on the back, so you can call them when it is time to pick up their posters. In schools have children put their room numbers on the back.)*

3. If desired, you can glue the posters to poster board to make them sturdier.

4. Display the posters for all to enjoy. Let children take them home at the end of the week.

Hints

You may want to let children create a practice drawing. When they are satisfied with this, they can create the actual poster.

Refrain from giving awards for "best" posters.

 Idea

Make these into sandwich boards and let kids wear them as they have a parade.

Song

"Oh How We Love the Library"

(Sung to: "Battle Hymn of the Republic")

Chorus:
Oh how we love the library.

Oh how we love the library.

Oh how we love the library.

It's filled with tons and tons and tons of great great stuff!

Verse 1:
There are stacks and stacks of books just waiting to be read.

There are videos to take and watch on your TV.

There are books with tapes and books on tape and cassettes too.

So, come to the library!

Repeat chorus

Verse 2:
There are toys, games and puzzles and computers too.

There are programs, activities and lots for you to do.

There are librarians who like to help you.

So, come to the library!

Repeat chorus

Adapt to fit your library.

Instructions for Creating Book Marks

Materials

- bookmark patterns on page 55
- crayons
- clear contact paper
- scissors

Directions

1. Give each child a copy of the bookmark patterns from page 55.

2. Have children color bookmarks using directions.

3. Have each child cut out their bookmarks. Provide assistance as needed.

4. Have children print their names on the back of their bookmarks. Assist those who need help printing.

5. Cover each child's bookmarks with clear contact paper. Let them take these home or keep them in their desks to use at school.

Instructions for Tour the Library

Materials

- 1 map of the library for each child

- stickers and/or stamps representing each department of the library. *(Each department should have an ample supply on hand for this activity.)*

Directions

1. Give each child a map of the library.

2. Tell children to "tour the library," visiting each department, where they will receive a sticker or a stamp.

3. As children visit each department, have someone from that department greet and welcome them warmly. The department representative can tell in a sentence of two what that department does.

4. The department representative(s) can give each child a stamp or sticker that represents the department. Have them put the stamp/sticker in the correct spot on the child's map.

5. When the child has visited all departments, they can return to the program area.

6. Children can take their maps home.

> **Hints**
>
> *Consider dividing the children into groups. Each group can visit the departments as a group.*
>
> *Stickers and stamps can include:*
> *Children's Dept.— book character sticker/stamp*
> *Adult Dept.— book stamp/sticker*
> *Magazines— magazine sticker/stamp*
> *Technical Services— computer sticker/stamp*
> *Audio Visual— AV-related sticker/stamp*
> *Community (Outreach) Services— bookmobile*
>   *sticker/stamp*
> *Circulation— date stamp*
>
> *Adapt this as needed for use in schools.*

Additional Activities

Something Old, Something New

Ask patrons (children and adults) to donate gently used books to the library. These should be in good condition, free of tears and marks. Donate these to a public or school library that has been destroyed or damaged by a natural disaster. You can also donate some of your discarded library books.

School Visits

Visit all schools that your library serves to advertise your summer reading program and activities. Perhaps several staff members can dress up to highlight the summer theme and prepare a humorous skit that will help promote summer reading. Design attractive flyers to give to each child. Ask the school newsletter editors to include information about the library's summer reading program in their end of the year newsletters. Make this an annual event. Schools can invite children's librarians to come and present a special program.

Books for Babies

Begin an ongoing service to give parents of newborns a board book for babies. Be sure to have several selections so that parents of multiples can have a different book for each baby. Put a library bookplate inscribed with the baby's name and date of birth inside each book. Make sure that parents know what programs and services you offer for children and families.

You can choose among these ideas or do one each day during National Library Week. Adapt as needed for use in school media centers.

Monday: Meet the Board Members and Director

Hold this informal social event in the evening when more people are likely to be available. Invite all members of the board and your director to "meet the public." Ask each board member wear a name badge that also lists their position on the board. Set up a table with refreshments (cookies and punch) in an area where board members can greet and visit with patrons.

Tuesday: Look Who's Here!

Have staff members dress up as famous fairy-tale characters. They can roam about the library telling children their stories and suggesting books for the children to read. Consider giving each child a large piece of card stock paper with artwork depicting this year's theme printed on it. They can get these autographed by the book characters. Perhaps the characters could give out stickers that represent their stories. Children can stick these on their autograph cards. Encourage parents to bring their cameras and take photos of their children with the book characters.

Wednesday: Bookmaking

Invite children to the library to create their own book. Let them use typing paper for the book pages. Children can write and illustrate their own original stories. Let them design an attractive cover with the story title and their name. Cover these with clear contact paper if desired. Use a paper punch to punch holes in the cover and pages. Attach them together with brackets. Keep in mind that children may not be able to write and illustrate their entire story in this one time slot. Give them several sheets of paper to take home.

An alternative is to make this a week-long project. Let children spend time each day working on their books. In schools, let each child read their stories to their classmates.

Thursday: Puppet Show

Present your own puppet show based on a children's book. An alternative is to hire an outside group to come in to present a puppet show. In schools, you can ask a class of older children to prepare and present a puppet show for the younger children.

Friday: Teachers and Principals Read Aloud Day

Invite teachers and principals to come to the library and read aloud to the children. Let them choose books they enjoy. In schools, have the principal visit each classroom and share a story with the children.

Saturday: Bookie Cookie Break

Host a "Bookie Cookie Break" for those families who participated in the "Read, Look and Listen" Program (pages 25–26). Have a program of storytelling, booktalking and music listening. This can be a good way to promote new materials. Encourage families to continue to read, look and listen together. Serve cookies shaped like book characters. Look in craft stores and home stores for a variety of cookie cutter shapes.

Read, Look and Listen!

Begin this program six to eight weeks before National Library Week. This is a family program where parents and children participate together. Each family can register as a family unit. Have them fill out the registration form below. Give each family one copy of the reporting form found on page 26. When they complete it and return it to you, they can have another form. Be sure to publicize this about a month before your program begins.

To complete each form each family must read one children's book together, listen to a children's book on tape or book/cassette packet (great for car rides), listen to a children's music cassette/CD and watch a video based on a children's book. Provide lists of videos that are based on children's books. Check nearby video stores to see what they offer, and let people know they can rent videos there as well as borrow them from the library.

Be willing to let families listen to music cassettes/CD's, books on tape or book/cassette packets in the library if they do not have this equipment at home. All you need is a tape or CD player and earphones. If possible, have a viewing room for families to watch a video together during this program.

On Saturday of National Library Week, have an "Bookie Cookie Break Program." See page 24 for details. Give each family who participates in the program an attractive certificate. If you want to give prizes, have families fill out a coupon for each form they return. Have a drawing where you give away a children's book, a children's book on tape, a children's music cassette/CD and a video based on a children's book.

READ, LOOK AND LISTEN REGISTRATION

Family's Last Name: _____

Parent's Names: _____

Children: Name   Grade   Age

_____   _____   _____

_____   _____   _____

_____   _____   _____

_____   _____   _____

_____   _____   _____

_____   _____   _____

Address: _____ City: _____

Zip Code: _____ Phone No: Area Code: _____ - _____ - _____

Parent Library Card Number: _____

Clip returned forms to this registration form or list returned forms on back.

Read, Look and Listen Report Form

Family's Last Name: _____ Phone Number: (____) ____ – _____

Parent's Names: _____

Children's Names: _____ _____

_____ _____

_____ _____

As a family, you must read one children's book, listen to one children's music cassette or CD, listen to one children's story on tape (or book/cassette packet) and watch one video based on a children's book. List each item you share together on this form. Tell us what you liked best about each and why you liked it. When your form is complete, return it to the Children's Department Reference Desk. You can complete as many forms as you choose, however you must enjoy one of each format listed on this form. We have lots of suggestions to offer, so if you need help, please ask us.

Book Title: _____ Author: _____

What we liked best about this book: _____

_____

Music Cassette/CD Title: _____ Composer: _____

What we liked best about this music cassette/CD: _____

_____

Book on Tape or Book/Cassette Title: _____ Author: _____

What we liked best about this story: _____

_____

Video Title: _____

Based on Book: _____ Author: _____

What we liked best about this video cassette: _____

_____

Celebrate Children's Book Week

Children's Book Week is celebrated in November. Check with the Children's Book Council (CBC) for exact dates and annual theme materials. A kick-off program is described below, with daily program suggestions for the rest of the week on page 34. Try to include the entire family in this celebration of books.

Kick Off Program (60–90 minutes)

Try to have this program on Sunday afternoon or the Monday that begins Children's Book Week. You can invite families to attend together.

The Children's Book Council offers kits that include posters, bookmarks and activity suggestions around each year's theme. Order early so you have plenty of time to plan (CBC address is on page 88). Choose stories, games, music and other activities that relate to the theme. Invite a local picturebook author or illustrator to participate in your celebration.

Welcome

The library director, school principal or librarian can offer a brief welcome and share ideas about how important reading is to us.

Story

Choose a story that highlights the theme of Children's Book Week.

Song

We Love to Read: Song found on page 30.

Poem

Look for a poem about books and reading. If it's humorous, that's even better.

Game

Something's Missing: Instructions are on page 29.

Story

Have your visiting author share one of their books.

Story

How a Picture Book Is Made: You or your visiting author can briefly tell how a picture book is written, illustrated and made into a book.

Story

Choose a book about reading or libraries to share with the children. Suggestions on page 29.

Project

Bookworm Bookmarks: Instructions are on page 30.

Booktalks

Highlight books about reading and books as well as books relating to this year's theme. Tell the story up to the climax without revealing the ending. Encourage children to check out the books and read them to discover how they end. An alternative is to have your visiting author "booktalk" their own books.

Activity

Give a Hand for Books: Instructions are on page 31.

Snacks

Give each person a cupcake and a cup of juice.

Closing

"Read Books" Cheer: Cheer is on pages 32–33.

Advertising Display

Use the posters and other promotional materials from the Children's Book Council to create an exciting display inviting people to celebrate Children's Book Week at the library.

Book Display

Have a display of children's books of yesteryear. These can often be found in used bookstores. Ask people in your community to loan or donate these books for a display. You can also display books that highlight this year's theme as well as other books about libraries, books and reading.

Room Decorations

Use the posters and other materials with this year's program kit. Select other decorations and paper goods that represent the theme. Have stuffed book characters from children's books displayed with their books. (For example, a monkey hanging above the Curious George books or Arthur Aardvark sitting near the Arthur Aardvark books.) Secure these well.

Name Tags

Use any self-stick name tags that represent this year's theme or reading and children's books. You can also use patterns from flannelboard books.

Snacks

Decorate a large round cake to resemble a bookworm's face. Add cupcakes in a variety of flavors and decorated in a variety of colored frostings to make a bookworm. Serve fruit juice for the beverage.

Special Guests

Invite the president of the library or school board, teachers, school principals, the mayor, etc., to share in your festivities.

Camera and Film

Have a camera loaded with a roll of color film. Take photos of your festivities, and display them later. Keep them in a scrapbook after you have finished displaying them. (See page 15 for starting a library scrapbook.)

Party Prizes (Optional)

Give each child a library or reading pin. If the Children's Book Council distributes one, consider using them. You might want to create your own pins to give to the children. Give out bookmarks that highlight the annual theme or other bookmarks related to books and reading.

Preliminary Activities

Favorite Books: Several months in advance, have each staff member write to five of their favorite, famous Americans. Explain that you are preparing for Children's Book Week to be celebrated during _____ (list dates).

Ask them to tell about the books they liked to read as children. Why were these their favorites? What do they enjoy reading to their children? And ask if they would send a photograph with their response. (See a sample letter on page 90.)

Famous Americans can include: the mayor, television personalities and sports figures (choose these with care), astronauts, the President of the United States and the First Lady, etc.

Laminate the responses you receive. Display the letters and photos on a large bulletin board or wall during Children's Book Week. Title this: *Favorite Books of Famous People.* You could also put them into sheet protectors and keep them in a large binder. When Children's Book Week is over, save these in a scrap book and keep them for patrons to enjoy.

Bookworm Cake

Program Resources

Asch, Frank. *Dear Brother.* Scholastic, 1992. Joey and Marvin find some old letters in the attic. They are enthralled to read about the adventures of their great uncles.

Bradby, Marie. *More Than Anything Else.* Orchard Books, 1995. More than anything, Booker T. Washington wants to learn to read.

Brown, Marc. *Arthur's Reading Race.* Random House, 1996. Arthur doesn't believe his little sister can read, but she surprises him.

Giff, Patricia Reilly. *The Beast in Ms. Rooney's Room.* Delacorte, 1986. Richard was having trouble in school until he got interested in reading. Then, he found a way to help his class.

Good Books, Good Times! Harper & Row, 1990 This book is filled with enjoyable poems about books and reading.

Hoban, Lillian. *Arthur's Prize Reader.* Harper & Row, 1978. Violet wins a great prize in the library reading contest.

Kehoe, Michael. *A Book Takes Root.* Carolrhoda Books, 1993. This book tells how a picture book is written, illustrated and produced.

————. *The Puzzle of Books.* Carolrhoda Books, 1982. This tells about the different people who help a book get published.

Levinson, Nancy Smiler. *Clara and the Bookwagon.* Harper & Row, 1988. Clara wants to learn to read, but her parents tell her reading is only for rich people. But, when the bookwagon comes to town, the librarian convinces Clara's parents that reading is for everyone.

McPhail, David M. *Edward and the Pirates.* Little, Brown, 1977. Once Edward learns to read, he has some amazing adventures.

Miles, Betty. *Hey, I'm Reading!* Knopf, 1995. This amusing book, makes learning to read lots of fun!

Materials and Prep

Instructions for Something's Missing Game

Materials

- a variety of dust jackets from children's books
- cover or card stock paper
- rubber cement
- laminating machine and film or clear contact paper
- scissors
- book related stickers *(one per child)*

Preparation

1. Laminate (or cover with contact paper) each book jacket.

2. Cut book jackets into puzzle pieces. Puzzles for preschool and kindergarten children can be cut into four squares or six rectangles.

    Puzzles for older children should be made more challenging by cutting irregularly shaped pieces.

3. After holding out a few pieces from each puzzle, put the puzzle jackets together. Glue these partially completed puzzles to card stock.

4. Hide the loose puzzle pieces in the library. Put pieces for *preschool and kindergarten children* in the picturebook section.

    Put pieces for *first and second graders* in the early reader section.

Put pieces for *third through fifth graders* in the middle grade fiction and nonfiction sections. Hide these very well. It's okay to challenge this age group.

6. Display the incomplete puzzles on the walls in your program area.

Directions

1. Show children the incomplete covers you displayed on the wall. Tell them that some of the pieces to the puzzle are missing. Without these pieces, we cannot tell which books these covers belong to.

2. Tell the children they should each look for *one* puzzle piece. Younger children may need assistance from staff, parents, guardians or older children.

3. When they find a piece, ask them to bring it back to the program area.

4. When everyone has returned, let each child come forward to try to find which puzzle their piece belongs to.

5. Give each child a sticker when they find the correct place for their puzzle piece.

Instructions for Making Bookworm Bookmarks

Materials

- glue
- darning needles

One per child of the following items:

- six 1" colored pom-poms
- three 36" pieces of yarn *(variety of colors)*
- two small movable eyes
- plastic sandwich bag
- blank white label

Preparation *(Do this prior to the program.)*

1. Cut yarn into strands 36 inches long.

2. Thread the needle with three strands at a time. Push the needle up through one pom-pom and back out the same side.

   You will then have six pieces of yarn hanging from the pom-pom. Make the ends even and then tie the yarn close to the pom-pom so it doesn't come loose. Make one of these per child.

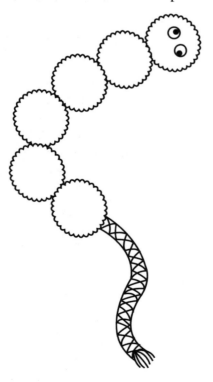

Directions

1. Give each child one pom-pom and two moveable eyes. Show the children how to glue the eyes to the pom-pom to create a face.

2. Give each child four more pom-poms. Have them glue the pom-poms together to make a worm. Then have children glue the head to the end of their worm.

3. Give each child one of the pom-poms with yarn strands. Show them how to braid the yarn to make a tail. Use two lengths for each part of the tail. Knot the yarn about two inches from the end.

4. Have the children glue the tail pom-pom to the other end of their bookworm.

5. Put each child's bookworm into a plastic sandwich bag. Label bags with the children's names.

Hint

Have parents and older children help younger children assemble their bookworms. Usually they just need someone to show them where to put the glue and where to glue each segment. Young children may need help with braiding the tail.

Song

"We Love to Read"

(Sung to: "Oh, When the Saints Go Marching In!")

We love to read! (clap, clap, clap, clap)

Oh, yes we do! (clap, clap, clap, clap)

We love to read those books together!

We love to read them every day!

We love to read all sorts of books! (clap, clap, clap, clap)

Sing this together several times, sing it as a round three times, and sing it once more together.

Instructions for Give a Hand for Books Bulletin Board

Materials

- heavy duty construction paper in a variety of colors
- black felt markers
- scissors
- staples and stapler
- pencils
- book jackets (use extras or color copy some)

Directions

1. Have the children take turns tracing each other's hands on construction paper.
2. Let the children cut out their hands.
3. Have each child print their first and last names on their hands.
4. Make a collage of book covers in the middle of the bulletin board
5. Place the children's hands around the edges of the board.
6. Add the bulletin board caption:
   Give a Hand for Books!

Hint

Provide assistance as needed with tracing, cutting and printing names.

 Idea

Take an instant photo of each child. Cut these so they fit inside the palm of the children's hand cutouts. Print each child's name on their hand.

Give a Hand for Books!

The Cheer for "Read Books!"

Materials

- 19 pieces of white poster board (12" x 12")

- bright colorful markers (*red, blue, purple, green work best*)

- pictures indicating different genres (*Try to make color photocopies of book covers from adventure, mystery, humor, family, sports, and animal stories.*)

- rubber cement

- laminating film and machine or clear contact paper

Additional Help

- 9 kids to be cheer leaders. They will hold up the Read Books cards

Preparation (*Do this prior to the program.*)

1. Print one letter from the words R E A D B O O K S on one side of each of the first nine pieces of poster board. Use large, thick capital letters that can be seen from a distance.

2. Glue one genre picture to each of the remaining pieces of poster board. Use markers to print the genre on the card.

3. Laminate all cards or cover with contact paper.

Directions

1. Choose nine children to be Cheer Leaders. Each child holds one letter from Read Books. They stand facing the "cheering section" (the other kids), so that the letters form the words *Read Books*.

2. Have them hold the cards in front of them, face down, so that the letters cannot be seen. Make sure that when they flip the cards up, the letters will appear right side up.

3. An adult or child assumes the role of Leader and leads the cheer on page 33.

4. Give "genre cards" to kids in the cheering section.

Additional Activities

Reading Is Important

Host a program for parents on the importance of reading to children. Discuss selecting age- and ability-appropriate books for children. Work with the schools PTA/PTO on programs to promote reading among children and their parents.

Cards for Kids

Encourage parents to get a library card for each of their children. Try to work with the schools on this program. Do your best to see that every child in your district has his or her own library card. Provide cards for children of all ages. Refrain from requiring children to be able to sign their name to be eligible. Design a card that is specifically for children.

A Treasure Chest of Books

Purchase a large treasure chest and fill it with paperback books on a variety of reading levels and topics. When children receive their first library card, let them choose a paperback from the treasure chest. Design a bookplate for your library so that you can enter children's names into their new book. Include children who move to the area and are getting their first library card at your library in this program. Advertise this in your library newsletter, local papers and in school newsletters. Be sure that circulation staff members know about the program so they can tell children who get new cards to stop by the children's reference desk to pick out their book.

Cheer for "Read Books!"

LEADER: Give us an R!

AUDIENCE: *R! (child holding "R" jumps out and holds card over head)*

LEADER: Give us an E!

AUDIENCE: *E! (child holding "E" jumps out and holds card over head)*

LEADER: Give us an A!

AUDIENCE: *A! (child holding "A" jumps out and holds card over head)*

LEADER: Give us a D!

AUDIENCE: *D! (child holding "D" jumps out and holds card over head)*

LEADER: Give us a B!

AUDIENCE: *B! (child holding "B" jumps out and holds card over head)*

LEADER: Give us an O!

AUDIENCE: *O! (child holding "O" jumps out and holds card over head)*

LEADER: Give us an O!

AUDIENCE: *O! (child holding "O" jumps out and holds card over head)*

LEADER: Give us a K!

AUDIENCE: *K! (child holding "K" jumps out and holds card over head)*

LEADER: Give us an S!

AUDIENCE: *S! (child holding "S" jumps out and holds card over head)*

LEADER: What should we do?

AUDIENCE: *READ BOOKS! (cheer leaders jump up with cards over heads)*

LEADER: What should we do?

AUDIENCE: *READ BOOKS! (cheer leaders jump up with cards over heads)*

LEADER: What should we do?

CHEER LEADERS: *R E A D   B O O K S (One at a time each cheer leader jumps up and shouts out their letter holding card high over head.)*

LEADER: What kinds of books? *(one at a time, each child in the "cheering section" will jump up high and hold their card over their head)*

KIDS: *Mysteries! Animal Stories! Nonfiction Books! Funny Books! Family Stories! Sports Stories! Adventure Stories! Biographies! School Stories!*

LEADER: What should we do?

ALL: *READ BOOKS! READ BOOKS! READ BOOKS! (This becomes a chant. Motion for kids to get softer and softer until they are whispering. Then let them get louder and louder until they are shouting.)*

ALL: *READING BOOKS IS FUN!!! (say three times)*

💡 Idea

You can add to this by letting kids call out favorite book titles. However, have them make these selections prior to the cheer, so that titles are appropriate and not repetitive. Let kids find a copy of their favorite book to hold up at the time they shout out their title.

There are programs for each day of Children's Book Week here. Do any or all of them, adapting them to fit your situation.

Sunday: Celebrate Children's Book Week

Kick off your week-long celebration with the special program found on page 27.

Monday: Meet the Author

Invite several local children's authors to visit your library or school. Invite them to present brief talks on their writing. Follow this with an autograph party. Children can bring one book for each author to sign. If possible, have books by those authors available for purchasing and autographing. While the authors are there, remember to have them sign the library's copies of their books. Add their autographed photos to your author's alcove (see page 52).

Tuesday: Children's Books of Yesteryear

Have a program where you highlight "Children's Books of Yesteryear." Tell the children how books of long ago were different from books we have today. Also talk about how books are similar. Choose some books to read to the children. Encourage them to share their thoughts and feelings about these books.

Wednesday: Let's Play

Have a children's theater group come and present a program based on children's books. Some of these groups do musical productions, others present programs involving audience participation. See what is available in your area. *Plan ahead and book early.* In schools, teachers can have individual classes prepare and present plays based on fairy tales. Let the children prepare the script, make the sets and costumes. These productions could be shared at small group assemblies throughout the day.

Thursday: "Let's Have a Parade"

Invite the children and staff to dress as their favorite storybook characters and have a parade. Since Children's Book Week comes so soon after Halloween, children most likely will be able to use their Halloween costumes. Have librarians, teachers and other staff members dress in costumes. Invite some favorite characters from children's books to attend (Little Red Riding Hood, Peter Pan and others). Let them tell "their" stories to the children. Have a costume parade through the building or neighborhood. Feel free to set standards for the types of costumes you wish to allow.

Friday: "Pajama Party"

Have an early evening Pajama Party. Invite children to come in their pajamas and listen to nighttime and bedtime stories. Have the staff members who are presenting the program dress in their pajama's too. You could also share books that highlight this year's theme. Encourage lots of variety in storytelling methods— flannelboard, reading aloud, telling, props, puppets, etc.

Saturday: "Game Day"

Provide a variety of board games based on books and reading. Include games on a variety of age and ability levels. Let children (and parents) spend time playing games together.

These might include standard board games such as Scrabble and Boggle. Learning games related to reading such as Consonants or Consonant Blends and Diagraphs (www.frankschaffer.com). There are also a number of games that have been made from popular children's books. These include: Goodnight Moon and Very Hungry Caterpillar (www.etoys.com); Green Eggs & Ham and The Cat in the Hat (www.universitygames.com); and Lilly's Purple Plastic Purse Game (www.gamewright.com).

Library Bookworms

This Bookworm program can be for children only, or it can be a family reading program where parents and children read together. Let each child or family fill out a colored circle for each book read. In schools, you can color code the bookworm segments by grade levels. (kindergarten, yellow; 1st grade, blue, etc.) Use the pattern below to make segments. As people turn segments in, start building your bookworm on a wall or bulletin board. See how long it grows to be. You can start this program in connection with Children's Book Week and have it conclude just prior to winter break. Invite those who participate to come to an "Eat the Library Bookworm" party with stories read by the school principal or librarian. Serve round cookies (bookworm segments) frosted with a variety of colored frostings. Arrange these to look like long bookworms. Adapt the registration form found on page 13.

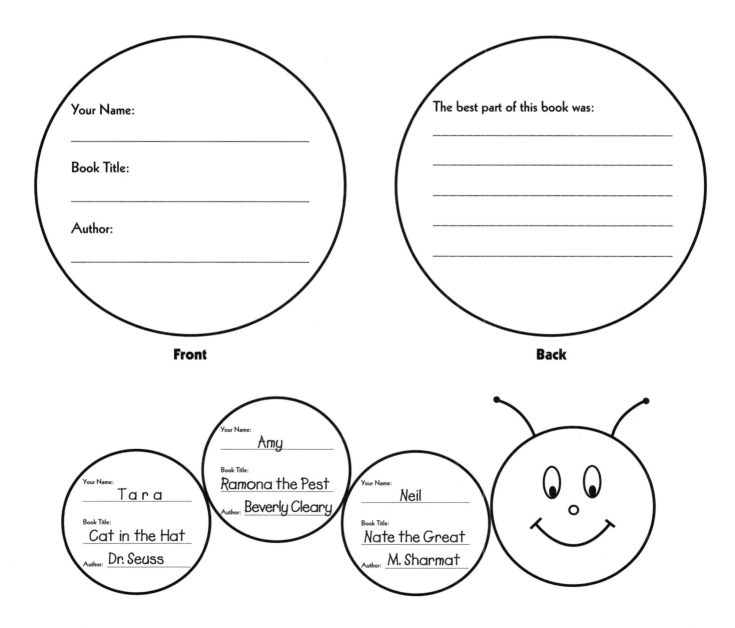

Your Name: _____

Book Title: _____

Author: _____

Front

The best part of this book was:
_____
_____
_____
_____
_____

Back

Your Name: Tara
Book Title: Cat in the Hat
Author: Dr. Seuss

Your Name: Amy
Book Title: Ramona the Pest
Author: Beverly Cleary

Your Name: Neil
Book Title: Nate the Great
Author: M. Sharmat

Celebrate Melvil Dewey's Birthday

Melvil Dewey created the Dewey Decimal Classification System. He was born December 10, 1851. Try to schedule his birthday party close to this date. Plan this program for children in grades one through five.

Program (60–90 minutes)

Welcome

Welcome the children to Melvil Dewey's birthday party. Mr. Dewey should knock on the door during the welcome. Open the door and say, "Hello, may I help you?"

Mr. Dewey: "I'm Melvil Dewey. I was told you needed my help."

Librarian: "Come on in Mr. Dewey. We do need your help, and we are having a birthday party for you!"

Mr. Dewey can act pleasantly surprised to learn that the children are celebrating his birthday.

Skit

The Mess of the Mixed-Up Books: Skit starts on page 38.

Game

Find These Books: Instructions are on page 40.

Project

Dewey Mobile: Instructions are on page 41–42.

Booktalks

Choose several books from each Dewey Decimal category and design a booktalk to highlight each. You might want to ask questions and encourage children to read in certain categories to discover the answers.

Activity

Sort It Out! Instructions are on page 41.

Song:

"The Books Are Lined Up on the Shelves" Song is on page 43.

Snacks

Light the candles on the cake and sing "Happy Birthday" to Mr. Dewey. Bring each child a piece of cake and a cup of juice.

Closing

Share a humorous poem about books and reading.

Planning and Promotion

Advertising Display

Create birthday cake with a book on top. Put a picture of Melvil Dewey on the cover. Print the program and registration information on the cake. Provide flyers for people to take as reminders.

Book Display

Have a variety of fiction and nonfiction books. Be sure to include a wide variety of subject areas. Encourage children to check these out on the day of the program.

Room Decorations

Decorate the room for a birthday party. Use a permanent black marker to print Dewey Decimal numbers on blown-up balloons. Glue Dewey Decimal numeral cutouts to the tablecloth. Have several piles of unsorted books on the floor and carts. They should not be in any order. The more mixed up they are the better. Look for posters depicting the different Dewey Decimal Classifications. Put posters on the proper shelves. When you list your Dewey Decimal numbers on the sides of the shelves, add a second sign that breaks down the numbers further (i.e., 636 Pets; 641 Cookbooks). This provides further assistance in locating books.

Name Tags

Choose any birthday or book-related self-stick name tags.

Snacks

Have a sheet cake decorated with books. Print HAPPY BIRTHDAY, MELVIN DEWEY! on it. Insert numeral candles to indicate Mr. Dewey's age.

Special Guests

Have a man on staff dress up and portray Melvil Dewey.

Camera and Film

Have a camera loaded with a roll of color film. Take photos of your program. Add them to your library scrapbook.

Party Prizes

Give each child a laminated bookmark that has the Dewey Decimal numbers printed on it.

Preliminary Activity

Hey, Mr. Dewey! Look Who's Reading!: Several weeks prior to the program, take photos of children reading in the library. Take photos of children and parents reading together, children sitting on the floor amid the stacks, children at tables, etc. Ask parents to bring photos of their children reading at home. Create a large bulletin board with the above title. Place a picture of Melvil Dewey in the center of the board. Surround it with the photos of the children reading. You can also include pictures of librarians, teachers and principals reading .

Program Resources

Fowler, Allan. *The Dewey Decimal System.* Children's Press, 1996. This book tells about Melvil Dewey and how he developed the Dewey Decimal System.

Gibbons, Gail. *Check It Out! The Book About Libraries.* Harcourt Brace Jovanovich, 1985. Gail Gibbons tells how libraries help us find good books.

Jaspersohn, William. *My Hometown Library.* Houghton Mifflin, 1994. The author tells how his hometown library helped him develop a love of books.

Knowlton, Jack. *Book and Libraries.* HarperCollins, 1991. This book highlights the development of written language, books and libraries.

Munro, Roxie and Julie Cummings. *The Inside Outside Book of Libraries.* Dutton, 1996. This book highlights several libraries throughout the U.S.

Ready, Dee. *Librarians.* Bridgestone, 1998. (Spanish, *Bibliotecarios y Bibliotecarias*, 1999) Learn about how librarians help you find the books and information you need.

The Mess of the Mixed-Up Books

This can be presented as a skit or a puppet show.

Characters: **Ima Bookbringer** (librarian with glasses perched on nose and gray hair in bun on top of head)

Page Turner (girl with braids and a flouncy dress)

Cliff Hanger (boy bouncing a ball)

Gotta Readmore (Swedish girl with blonde hair and dress)

Melvil Dewey (young man in suit)

Setting: a library

Era: late 1800s

Ima Bookbringer is sitting at a desk. Around her are messy piles of books. The shelves are a disaster. Some books are sorted by colors, others by size. Melvil Dewey is seated at a table near the reference desk. He is surrounded by a pile of books and papers. He is busy writing something with a quill pen. Cliff Hanger enters the library bouncing a ball and walks over to the desk.

Cliff: Hi, my name is Cliff Hanger. I have to do a report for school.

Ima: You've come to the right place Cliff. What's your report about?

Cliff: Some guy named Christopher Columbine or something like that. My teacher says he's an explorer or something.

Ima: Oh, you mean Christopher Columbus. Let me see what I can find. They don't call me Ima Bookbringer for nothing, you know. *(Ima walks over to the shelves, and starts to look around.)*

Let's see now. I saw a book about Christopher Columbus just yesterday. I think it was tall and blue. *(She looks through the tall books and the blue books, but she can't find it. She walks back over to Cliff.)* I'm sorry, I can't find a book about Christopher Columbus. Would a book on George Washington do? Or how about Paul Revere?

Cliff: No. It has to be Christopher Columbine. Somebody else already has those other guys. Well thank you anyway, Mrs. Bookbringer. *(Cliff exits. Page Turner enters.)*

Ima: This place is a real mess. There has to be a better way to organize books.

Page: Excuse me. Could you please help me find a book? It was a really good book about a dog. And I want to do it for a book report in school.

Ima: I sure can! They don't call me Ima Bookbringer for nothing, you know! Now tell me more about this book you are looking for. Have you read it before? And tell me your name too. I like to know the names of people I help.

Page: Page Turner. The book is about a dog. It was a brown dog, but I forgot its name.

Ima: Do you know the names of the other characters in the story?

Page: I forgot. But I think I remember what the book looks like. It's green and it's kinda long and I think it has a dog on the front of it. Or maybe it has a boy and a dog on it.

Ima: Well, let me see what I can find.

Page: Would you like me to help you look?

Ima: Oh no, Page. You might get things all mixed up. We'd never let patrons look for books by themselves. *(Ima looks around. Finally she finds several long green books, but only one has a dog on it.)* Look, here it is! Here's a green book with a dog on the front.

Page: No, that's not the same book. The dog was different.

Ima: Well, why don't you try these books. Maybe you can use one of them for your report.

Page: No, thank you. I really want to find that book. Good bye. *(Page exits.)*

Ima: This sure isn't my day for finding books. There has to be a better way to organize books. *(Gotta Readmore enters, skipping to the desk.)*

Gotta: Hello, my name is Gotta Readmore. My family and I, we just moved here from Sweden, and my teacher wants me to find a book about America.

Ima: You've come to the right place, Gotta. They don't call me Ima Bookbringer for nothing. Let me see what I can find. *(She looks through stack after stack of books, but she can't find any books on America. She comes back with books on other countries.)* Well, I guess the books on America are checked out, or maybe they are in some other stacks somewhere. But I found some books about France and Germany.

Gotta: No, thank you. I know about those countries. I have to learn about America. *(Gotta exits.)*

Ima: I haven't been able to help one person today. There has to be a better way to organize these books.

Melvil: *(Melvil Dewey gets up from the table and carries his papers and pen to the desk.)* Excuse me, Mrs. Bookbringer. My name is Melvil Dewey. I've been noticing that you have been having trouble finding the right books.

Ima: I sure have. There has to be a better way to organize these books.

Melvil: I'm a librarian too, and I've had the same problem.

Ima: You are? You have?

Melvil: I'm working on a method that will help people find library books. It's called the Dewey Decimal System. The books will be organized by subject. All of the books about the same subject will be shelved together. Each subject will have a Dewey Decimal Number. The books will be in numerical order. Fiction books will be shelved alphabetically by the author's last name, so all of the books by one author will be together. There will be a card catalog. You will be able to look up books by their title, subject or author. I still have a lot of work to do on it, Mrs. Bookbringer, but I'm confident that the Dewey Decimal System will revolutionize libraries.

Ima: I have a feeling the world will remember you for a long time, Mr. Dewey.

Instructions for Find These Books

Materials

- 1 list of 12 topics per child. (*Make these age/grade appropriate. There should be one book per Dewey class, one fiction title and one biography. See sample below.*)

- 1 paper bag per child

Additional Help

- staff or volunteers to help children look up books in the catalog

Directions:

1. Give each child a list of topics.

2. Tell children to look up each topic in the catalog and write the call number on the line provided.

3. Encourage the children to find a book with that call number and put it into their bags.

4. When they have found all of the books on their list, they can return to the librarian or teacher to have their items checked.

Hints

Adapt this to meet your library's setup.

Be willing to provide assistance as needed.

Have staff and volunteers work with groups of first through third graders. Each group of three to five children can work with an adult who will help them use the catalog to look up their topics and help them find books. Each child in the group can choose one book per topic to put into their bags.

You could also have older students who are proficient at library skills provide assistance to younger children.

Sample Topic List for Grades 4–5

1. Look for a book about dreams. _____

2. Look for a myth (or Bible story, etc.). _____

3. Look for a book about money (or costumes, government, etc.). _____

4. Look up Spanish Language Books (or other languages, dictionaries, etc.). _____

5. Look up elephants (or whales, monkeys, dinosaurs, etc.). _____

6. Find a book about the Space Shuttle (or buildings, dogs, cats, etc.). _____

7. Look up baseball (substitute other sports, crafts, magic tricks, etc.). _____

8. Look up poetry, and find a book of poems to read. _____

9. Look up Illinois (or other states or historical topics). _____

10. Look for a biography. Choose anyone you like. _____

11. Find a fiction book by your favorite author. _____

12. Find an encyclopedia. _____

Materials and Prep

Instructions for Sort It Out

Materials

- several carts of unsorted library books
- whistle
- library stickers

Directions

1. Divide children into groups of four. Have two kids stand on each side of the library cart.

2. Show the children how library pages sort books on the book cart before they shelve them.

3. Now, blow the whistle and let the kids have a turn at sorting a book cart of books.

4. Give each child a library sticker when they correctly complete their sorting. See that everyone gets a sticker.

Hints

This is not a contest to see who "wins." What is important is getting it right.

Vary the difficulty level according to grade and ability level of children.

First through third graders could have a cart with one book from each category and five fiction books, each author beginning with a different letter of the alphabet, and three biographies each person beginning with a different letter of the alphabet.

Fourth and fifth graders could have a cart with two or more books from each category and ten fiction books with some authors names beginning with the same letter of the alphabet and five biographies.

Instructions for Dewey Mobile

Materials

- colored markers *(fat and thin tipped)*
- hole puncher

One each of the following items per child

- one 3" card stock circle with a picture of Melvil Dewey glued to it. Print Melvil Dewey under the picture. Print "The Dewey Decimal System" on the back of the circle. Punch a hole in the top of this circle.

- twelve 3" card stock circles *(use as many colors as possible)*

- glue stick or glue bottle

- two 6" strands of colored yarn

Directions

1. Give each child one circle. Have them print *000* in the center of the circle. Under the number have them print *Generalities*. Let them draw a picture of something that represents that category on the back of the circle. Provide ideas. Punch a hole in the top of the circle and attach a piece of yarn. Tie it at the top. Punch a hole in the bottom of that circle.

2. Do the same thing for each category, but *don't* punch holes in these circles.

3. Have the children glue their circles together to make a wreath. The numbers should go in clockwise order.

4. Use the second strand of yarn to attach the circle with Mr. Dewey's picture to the 000 circle (see illustration on page 42).

Illustration of Dewey Mobile

Drawings of each category are on the back of each circle.

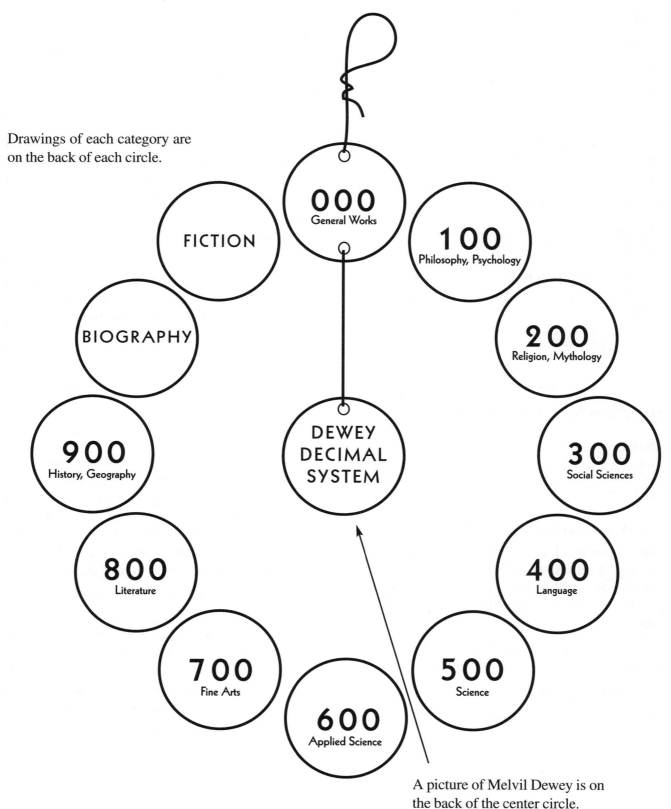

A picture of Melvil Dewey is on the back of the center circle.

"The Books Are Lined Up on the Shelves"
(Sung to: "The Ants Go Marching")

The books are lined up on the shelves, hurrah, hurrah
The books are lined up on the shelves, hurrah, hurrah
Mr. Dewey helped with the books
It's really much easier than it looks,
And the books are lined up on the library shelves.

First you have the General stuff, hurrah hurrah
Their numbers all begin with zero, hurrah, hurrah.
Computers, news, so much to do
Encyclopedias are found here too
And the books are lined up on the library shelves.

The ones come next on the shelves, hurrah, hurrah
Psychology, philosophy, hurrah, hurrah
Ghosts and dreams and logic are here
Once you learn it, it's really quite clear,
And the books are lined up on the library shelves.

The twos come next on the shelves, hurrah, hurrah
Books on religion and myths are here, hurrah, hurrah
Lots of stories to read and enjoy
Something for every girl and boy,
And the books are lined up on the library shelves.

The threes come next on the shelves, hurrah, hurrah
Clothing and customs are found here, hurrah, hurrah
Planes and trains and things that go
Money, law and good stuff to know
And the books are lined up on the library shelves.

The fours come next on the shelves, hurrah, hurrah
Languages and words to learn, hurrah, hurrah
You'll find dictionaries and thesaurus too
Help with spelling and words for you
And the books are lined up on the library shelves.

The fives come next on the shelves, hurrah, hurrah
Science books are found here, hurrah, hurrah
Animals, biology,
Chemistry, astronomy,
And the books are lined up on the library shelves.

The sixes come next on the shelves, hurrah, hurrah
More science books for you to read, hurrah, hurrah
Pets and cooking, buildings too.
Lots of fun, so much to do,
And the books are lined up on the library shelves.

The sevens come next on the shelves, hurrah, hurrah
Filled with lots of fun for you, hurrah, hurrah
Sports and crafts and magic to do
Things to do at your parties too,
And the books are lined up on the library shelves.

The eights come next on the shelves, hurrah, hurrah
Lots of good stuff for you to read, hurrah, hurrah
Poetry and plays to read
See if you can read them with speed,
And the books are lined up on the library shelves.

The nines are next on the shelves, hurrah, hurrah
Filled with stuff for you to learn, hurrah, hurrah
History, geography
Facts about state and country,
And the books are lined up on the library shelves.

Then we have biographies, hurrah, hurrah
What interesting stories they can be, hurrah, hurrah
The stories about the people are true
Learn about the great things they do,
And the books are lined up on the library shelves.

Then there are the fiction books, hurrah, hurrah
In author order A to Z, hurrah, hurrah
Mysteries, adventures too
Stories about kids like you,
And the books are lined up on the library shelves.
HURRAH! (Shout it! Raise arms!)

Sing the final line slowly until you get to the word *up*.
Then sing the phrase *on the library shelves* rapidly,
ending with a shouted *Hurrah!*

Books! Books! Books!

Each child must read one book from each subject area, and one biography and one fiction book from each genre. Give each child copies of Number Please/Read to Learn on pages 65–66 and Fiction Fun on page 60. Adapt the registration form on page 13. Children may choose whichever books they want as well as what reporting methods to use.

Schools can set aside time each week for children to share book reports and projects. Both schools and libraries can display the children's projects. At the end of the program, each child who completed both the nonfiction and fiction requirements can be invited to a Pizza, Pop and Popsicles Party with the principal or librarian who will read or tell their favorite stories.

To make this more enjoyable create a large spinner. Paint each segment a different color and label it with a Dewey category (000s 100s, etc.). Children can spin the spinner to find out what kind of book they should read next. For fiction books create a large square inside a box with sides. Draw a map of various "reading lands" (adventure, mystery, etc.—use the same designations that are on the chart on page 60.). Each child will be able to toss a small stone inside the box. The "land" they visit will tell them what kind of book to read. Make the map colorful and fun.

This can be an ongoing program that begins just before winter break and ends in May.

Additional Activities

Library Skills

Develop a library skills program for third or fourth graders. Create a live action video presentation or puppet slide/sound show about how to use your library. You'll need to write a script, create puppets, and costumes. Make this humorous and fun as well as instructional. Design a booklet that highlights the program. The booklet can include a variety of library exercises that will help children look up and find different kinds of materials in the library. Children who successfully complete their booklets can be given a special pin.

Rollin' Library

Arrange to visit as many classes as possible to present age and grade level appropriate booktalks. You can plan booktalks for kindergarten/grade 1, grades 2–3, grades 4–5 and Junior High. Design clever bookmarks listing all books and call numbers used for each booktalk.

When you present your booktalk, be sure never to reveal any endings. Tell the story up to the climax. Then tell the children if they want to find out how the book ends, they must come to the library and check it out. Be sure to have plenty of copies on hand. Try to avoid some of the "pop culture series" books and highlight other books you'd like to introduce to the kids. Be prepared for lots of kids at the library after a school appearance.

You can make a wagon look like an old fashioned bookmobile. Put your supplies in it, and you're a rollin' library.

Booksharing

Ask patrons to donate new or gently used paperback books for contribution to the local homeless shelters.

And the Winner Is

Award-Winning Books

The Newbery, Caldecott, Golden Kite and Hans Christian Andersen are among the many awards given to children's books. This program is for a Caldecott or Newbery Award, however it can be adapted to highlight any award you choose. You might use it to honor your library's awards. See page 52 for details on starting your own awards program.

Program (60–90 minutes)

Welcome

Share a poem about books and reading. You can create your own or use one from a book.

Awards Ceremony

Explain the significance of the award you are highlighting. Then announce the book(s) receiving this year's award. Show the book(s) to the children. If an award sticker is available, add it to the book.

Story

Read or tell the winning story.

Author Talk

Provide a brief talk about the winning author or illustrator.

Activity

Create a Banner: Instructions are on page 47.

Song

We Love to Read Song is on page 30. Adapt it to fit your program.

Booktalks

Booktalk the honor (runner up) books. You could also highlight other books by the winning author or illustrator.

Art Project

Reading Star Mobiles: Instructions are on pages 47–48.

Story

Share another book from this year's winners.

Bookmark Awards

Announce the winner in your Design a Bookmark Contest. See page 50–51 for details.

Snacks

Bring each child a cookie and a cup of hot chocolate.

Closing

Read Books! Cheer: Instructions are on page 33. Adapt this to fit reading award-winning books.

Advertising Display

Design a poster that features a drawing of the award. Print COME TO A _____ AWARD CELEBRATION on the poster. Include program dates, time and registration information. Provide flyers for people to take as reminders. Decorate the poster with stars.

Book Display

Provide a book display that features all of the award books in that category. Add this year's winners at the conclusion of the program.

Room Decorations

Decorate the room with red, white and blue award ribbons, stars, balloons, etc. Try to find book-related decorations (mobiles, posters, etc.).

Name Tags

Have star-shaped name tags. Print the child's first and last name on the tag. (Pattern on page 48.)

Snacks

Have star-shaped sugar cookies frosted in a variety of colors. Serve hot chocolate.

Special Guests

If you have any award-winning authors in your area, invite them to your celebration.

Camera and Film

Have an instant camera loaded with film. Take an instant photo of each child upon arrival. Also take photos of your program, and display them later. Then add them to your scrapbook (see page 15).

Party Prizes (Optional)

Create a bumper sticker that says, "I'm a ★ reader!" Add your library's name. Have these printed up, and give one to each child who attends the program.

Preliminary Activity

Design a Bookmark Contest: Sponsor a Design a Bookmark Contest in which children design a bookmark that highlights an award-winning book. Have children use a no. 2 pencil to design their bookmarks. Go over the lines in black felt pen before you print the bookmark. Choose one winner from each grade level (or classroom).

Children can be given a packet of one hundred of their own bookmarks plus one of each of the other winners. Print additional bookmarks to be distributed in the library. Print bookmarks on different colors of card stock so that each winner's work is special. Try to gather all winners for a group photo holding their winning bookmarks. Announce the winners at the program, an assembly, your newsletter and area newspapers. Give winners a special certificate or ribbon. A pattern, entry sheet and contest rules are on pages 50–51.

Program Resources

These books tell about the various book awards given to children's authors and illustrators.

Award-Winning Books for Children and Young Adults: An Annual Guide. Scarecrow Press, 1990.

Children's Book, Awards and Prizes. Children's Book Council, 1969--.

Children's Writers and Illustrators Market. Writer's Digest Books, annual.

Jones, Dolores Blythe. *Children's Literature Awards and Winners.* Neal-Schuman, 1988.

Internet Resources:

From the *Yahoo* page (yahoo.com) follow this path to find information on authors.

Arts & Humanities--Literature--Authors--Children's

Follow this path for information on awards:

Arts & Humanities--Literature--Awards--Children's

Instructions for Create a Banner

Materials

- 1 computer generated banner that says *CONGRATULATIONS! (Choose a font that outlines the letters.)*
- crayons, markers, pencils
- mailing tube

Directions:

1. Lay the banner out on the table.
2. Allow children to color in the letters on the banner. Each child can also draw a small picture and write a brief message of congratulations.

3. Write a letter to the author(s) who received this year's award telling about your program. Explain that the children created this banner to show their appreciation for the books they write. Put the banner and letter into the mailing tube and send it to the author(s). When you receive a reply, display the author's letter along with photos you took of the program and the author's books.

 Idea

Send banners to the honor book winners too. You can divide a large group into smaller groups and have each group work on a separate banner.

Instructions for Reading Star Mobiles

Materials

- 1 large star per child (pattern on p. 48)
- three small stars per child (pattern on p. 48)
- child's photo (*child can use school photo or one taken at the event*)
- yarn
- pencils
- glue
- paper punch
- glitter
- crayons

Preparation

1. Punch holes in the top and bottom of the large star. String top hole with yarn.
2. Punch a hole in the top of each small star. Punch a hole in the bottom of two of the small stars.

Directions

1. Give each child a large star.
2. Have children use black marker to print their name on the back of the large star.
3. Give each child their photo and have them glue it in the center of the front of the large star.
4. Outline the edges of the star with glitter.
5. Give children three small stars and yarn. Let them fill out the information on each star and use crayons and glitter to decorate them. Show them how to attach the stars with yarn so they hang vertically.

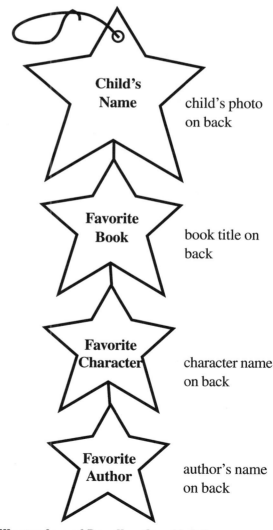

Illustration of Reading Star Mobile

Patterns for Nametag, Reading Program and Star Mobile

Enlarge or reduce patterns as needed.

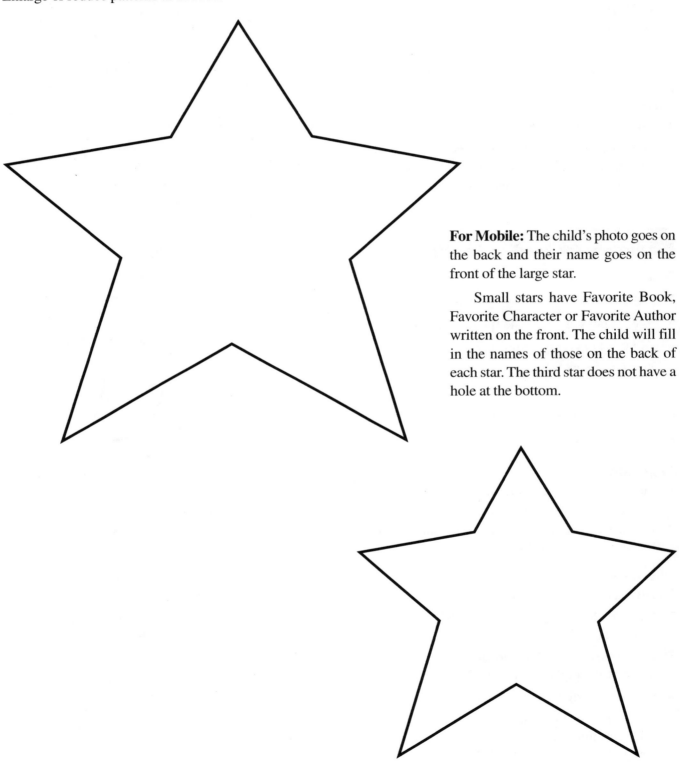

For Mobile: The child's photo goes on the back and their name goes on the front of the large star.

Small stars have Favorite Book, Favorite Character or Favorite Author written on the front. The child will fill in the names of those on the back of each star. The third star does not have a hole at the bottom.

Reach for the Stars

Design a reading program that encourages children to read award-winning books, listen to award-winning tapes and watch award-winning videos. Apply self-stick stars to the spines of award-winning books, audiocassettes and videos. You might want to color code them (Newbery, red; Caldecott, blue; Golden Kite, gold and so on) or you can put any color star on any award winners you choose. Keep lists of all award winners at the children's reference desk. Keep in mind that some books win several awards. Be sure to make note of this.

Give each child a star cutout (sample below). Children can fill out one star for each award-winning title they complete. Audiotapes and videos made of award-winning books are counted as award winners.

There are awards given to music cassettes too, so be sure to include these.

Attach string to returned stars and hang them from the ceiling. Invite all children who participate in the program to A Stars Come Out Party where they can be awarded a star-shaped pin that says, **Star Reader**. Perhaps you can have a local author come and present a special program. If you have an award-winning author nearby, all the better. Alternatives are to present a puppet show or play based on award-winning children's books.

Report Forms

You can fill out one star for each award-winning book you read, award-winning tape you listen to or award-winning video you watch. Cut out the star and fill out the front. Write a brief review of the "award winner" you selected on the back. Return it to the librarian who will hang it up for you. You can read, watch or listen to as many award books, videos or cassette tapes as you choose.

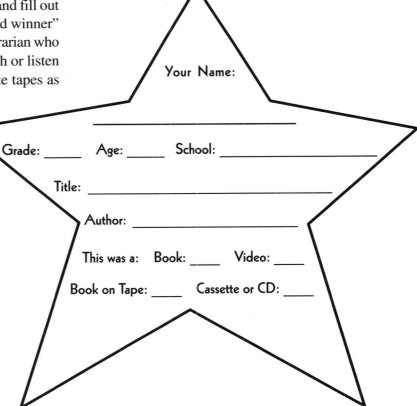

Your Name:

_____

Grade: _____ Age: _____ School: _____

Title: _____

Author: _____

This was a: Book: _____ Video: _____

Book on Tape: _____ Cassette or CD: _____

Rules for Design a Bookmark

Use the outline on the next page to design a bookmark. Read these rules carefully before you begin.

1. This must be your own artwork. You cannot have help from another person, the computer or a pattern book.

2. You must design a bookmark that highlights an award-winning book. See the librarian for help in finding an award winner you wish to highlight.

3. Use a no. 2 pencil to draw your picture and print the title of the book and the author's first and last name on the bookmark.

4. Fill out the information on the bookmark form.

5. Return this paper to the librarian (your teacher).

6. There will be one winner from each grade level (class). Winners will be announced on _____ (date). Each winner will receive a packet of one hundred of their own bookmarks, plus one each of the other winning bookmarks. A certificate (ribbon) will be given to each winner.

Design a Bookmark Entry Form

Your Name: _____   _____
                         (first)   (last)

Address: _____

Phone Number: (_____) _____ - _____   Library Card Number: _____

School: _____

Grade: _____   Teacher: _____   Room Number: _____

Book: _____

Author: _____

. . . .

I have designed this bookmark by myself without help from another person, a computer or pattern book. I have read and understand the rules of this contest.

_____

Sign your name on the line above.

I certify that my child has designed his/her own bookmark without the help from another person, a computer or pattern book. My child has my permission to participate in this contest. I have read and I understand the rules that accompany this entry form.

_____

Parent's signature

Design a Bookmark

Use the outline below to design your bookmark. Fill in the information on the attached form. Make a copy of your bookmark and the registration information. Entries will not be returned.

Please leave this space blank. If your bookmark wins,
your name & grade will go here.

Create Your Own Awards Program

Design a book and audiocassette awards program for your school or library. These awards can be given on an annual basis. Design a sticker that can be used to identify the award winners in your collection. Also design a certificate that can be sent to the author, illustrator or composer to notify them of the award.

Getting started

Name your award.

Decide on criteria. Choose five items in any or all of the following categories: Picture Book (include story and illustrations in the same award), Early Reader, Middle Grade Fiction, Biography, Non-Fiction, Poetry, Music Cassette, Story Cassette, Children's Video.

Nominate titles. Have those who select and review in each category nominate five titles from their categories. Make out a list. Materials should be items published in the previous year. (For example in the year 2000, you will give awards to materials published in 1999.)

Have children vote. Ask children in your school or library district to vote on their favorites. Those voting must read or listen to all five nominations in each category they vote in. Keep copies on reserve in the library for patrons to preview there. Also have copies for circulation. Provide the schools (or public libraries) in your district with copies of your award contenders, so they can make these available to the children.

Announce the award winners at the award program. Be sure to add stars to these materials.

Author's Alcove

Select a corner of the learning center or children's department to become an Author's Alcove. Have staff members write letters to children's authors asking them to tell what their favorite children's books are and who their favorite children's authors are. Ask for an autographed photo too. Frame the letters and photos when they arrive, and display them on the wall. Add a cozy seating arrangement and an attractive, eye-catching shelf display. Display books by the author's who are part of your Author's Alcove. Make note of those who are local authors.

And the Winners Are

Compile an ongoing list of award-winning books. Add to it each year as annual winners are announced. Keep this in a binder. Use subject dividers to highlight each award. List the winners by year. Include author, title, call number and a brief annotation for each book. Make this available for patrons to use. This will be a valuable source when children and adults studying children's literature need to find award-winning books. Keep a separate copy for staff use.

Puzzles and Activities

How to Use Puzzles & Activities in This Section

This section contains a variety of puzzles and other activities related to libraries, books and reading. Some encourage children to check out library materials (book, cassette, video, etc.), enjoy them and return to tell you about them. There are two puzzles designed to be used as reading logs. One is for nonfiction, the other fiction. Both require children to read a particular kind of book, but at the same time they give children the choice of which book in that area to read. These can also be used for read aloud programs where parents read to children. Upon completion of some puzzles, children are encouraged to return to the library to receive something special (stamp, sticker, bookmark, etc.) Giving rewards of course is optional.

You can use these puzzles in a variety of ways:

- As a part of each of the celebrations in this book. Put one or two different puzzles out per day. Encourage children to design their own covers and make these into a booklet of puzzles and activities.

- To create the *Library Activity Book* found in Welcome to Your Library (page 15).

- To encourage children to enjoy a variety of library materials and genres.

When using puzzles with children, feel free to adapt them to meet the individual needs of the students you are working with.

- Consider making separate *Library Activity Books* for each age grouping (preschool--kindergarten, grades 1–2, grades 3–5). Include age-appropriate activities and puzzles in each book. Design an attractive cover for each, and run the covers on different colors of paper.

- For coloring puzzles, add lines to make puzzles more challenging or erase lines to make them easier.

- Connect the dots on dot-to-dot puzzles. Use them as coloring pages.

- Draw a line thru mazes. Let children trace over them or color the path.

- Fill in parts of the puzzles, and let children complete them.

- Divide the children into groups. Each person can compete one portion of the puzzle.

- Complete the puzzle as a group.

Create puzzles of your own that feature your own library, and the library skills you wish to teach. You can add these to the *Library Activity Book*.

Keep in mind, that these puzzles are designed for fun, and to make learning about the library an enjoyable experience.

Note: The following puzzle pages are designed to run back to back: 65-66, 74-75 and 82-83.

We're Lost

Help the kids find their way to the town library.

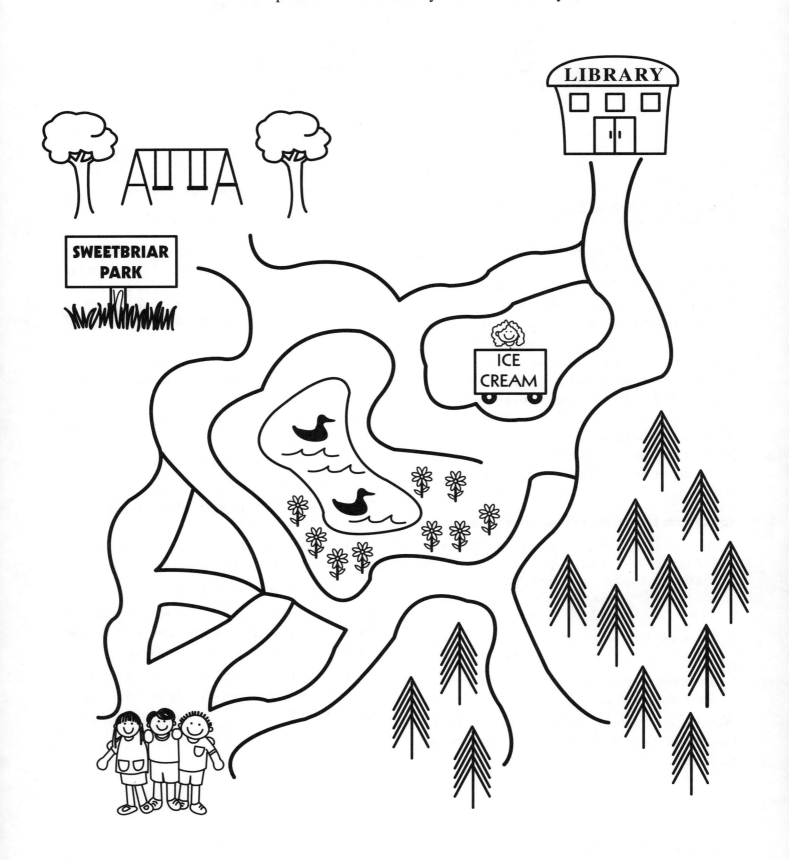

Bookmark Designers

Design some bookmarks. Color: B=Blue, R=Red, Y=Yellow, G=Green, O=Orange
When you are finished, cut out the two bookmarks. Then cover them with clear contact paper.

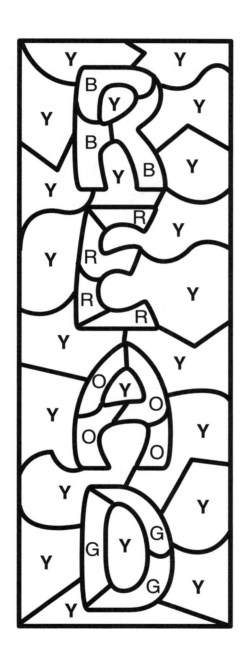

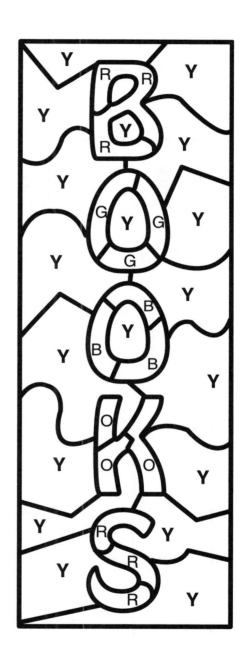

A Great Place to Go

Connect the dots to discover a great place you can go to find books, cassettes, videos, programs and much more. Color your picture.

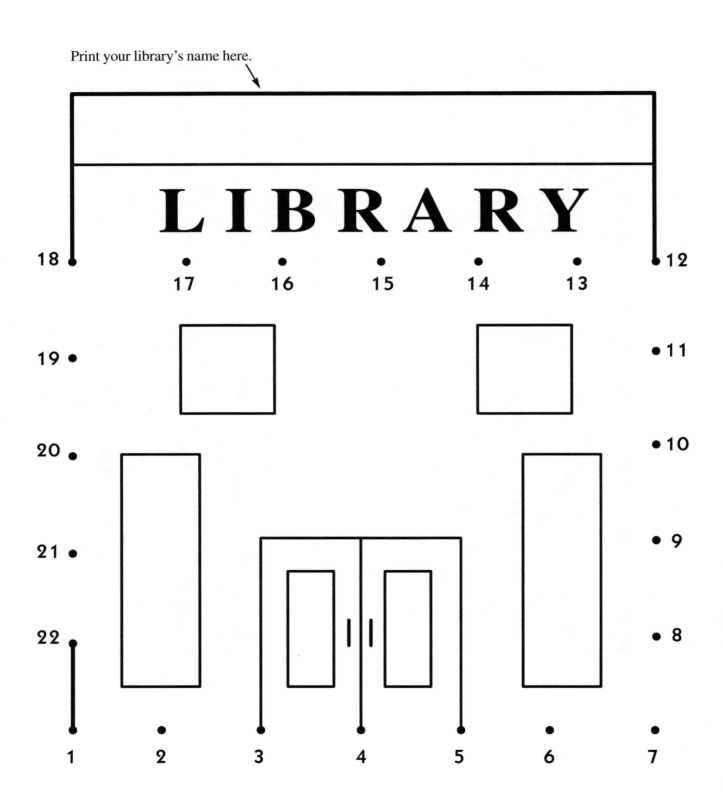

Print your library's name here.

LIBRARY

What's There?

Follow the letter path to find these words. Circle each word as you find it. When you are finished you will have some letters left over. What is the message they spell out?

___ ___ ___ ___ ___ ___ ___ ___ ___ ___ ___ ___ ___ ___ ___ ___ ___!

Books	Computers	Fun	Homework	Kids
Cassettes	Reading	Learning	Puzzles	Librarians
Videos	Programs	Magazines	Information	

INFORMATIONUBOOKSSFUNEHOMEWORKYCOMPUTERSOREADINGUCASSETTESRLEARNINGLMAGAZINESIPROGRAMSBPUZZLESRKIDSALIBRARIANSRVIDEOSY

Where Do We Go?

These kids can't find the children's room in their library. Can you help them?

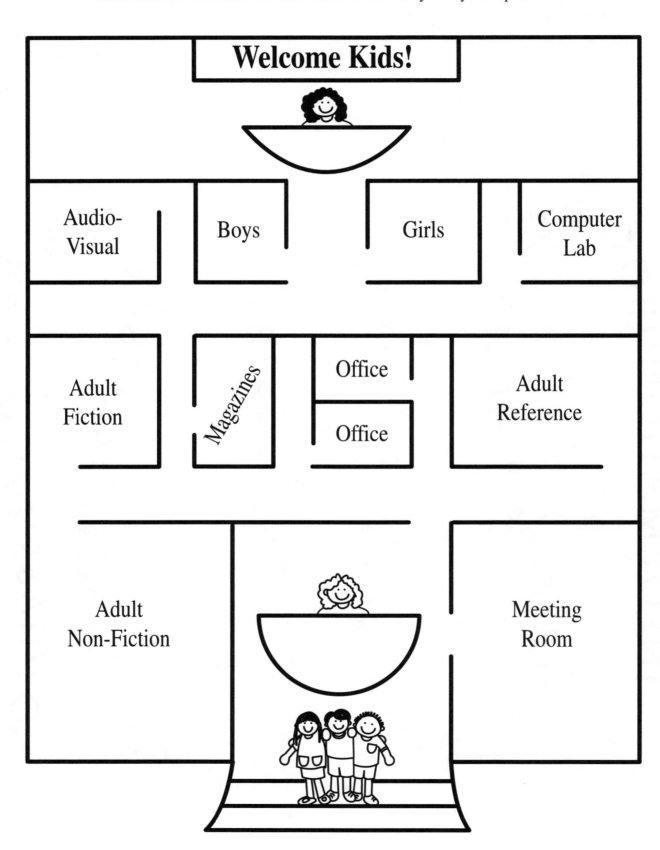

Welcome Kids!

Audio-Visual

Boys

Girls

Computer Lab

Adult Fiction

Magazines

Office

Office

Adult Reference

Adult Non-Fiction

Meeting Room

Read It!

Color: B=Blue, G=Green, Y=Yellow, O=Orange, L=Lavendar, W=Brown, R=Red, P=Purple, U=Light Blue, N=Light Green

When you find out what these are, check one out. Take it home and read it. Bring it back and tell the librarian about it. You will receive a special stamp.

Fiction Fun

There are many types of fiction books. Unscramble the words below to find out what they are. Then select a fiction book about every subject. We'll be glad to help you find books to read. Just ask! Print the titles in the spaces provided. Bring your completed "reading log" to your teacher or librarian. Choose one of these reporting methods tell about your book. You must use each method at least once, but you may choose which method to use for which book. A. Make a poster to advertise your book. B. Present an oral "booktalk" about your book. Remember when giving a booktalk, you cannot reveal how the book ends. C. Design and write a newspaper article about one of the events in the book. D. Make a mobile that highlights events in the story. E. Write a letter to the author telling why you liked this book.

STORPS __ __ __ __ __ __

Title: _____

MALSANI __ __ __ __ __ __ __

Title: _____

TERYMYS __ __ __ __ __ __ __

Title: _____

NCESCIE TIONFIC __ __ __ __ __ __ __ __   __ __ __ __ __ __ __

Title: _____

ROHUM __ __ __ __ __

Title: _____

FYLIMA __ __ __ __ __ __

Title: _____

VENTUREAD __ __ __ __ __ __ __ __ __

Title: _____

YRIAF ELAT __ __ __ __ __   __ __ __ __

Title: _____

KOLF LATE __ __ __ __   __ __ __ __

Title: _____

HOOSCL __ __ __ __ __ __

Title: _____

Check It Out!

Color: P=Purple, R=Red, G=Green, Y=Yellow, O=Orange, L=Lavendar, B=Blue, K=Pink, A=Gray.
Now find one of these and listen to it in the library or check it out to enjoy at home. Tell us about it, and we'll give you a sticker.

What Did They Write?

Look up these authors in the catalog. Next to their names, print the title of one of their books. Now go to the shelf and try to find that book. Remember that fiction books are filed alphabetically by the last name of the author. Bring this sheet and the books to the librarian, who will give you a sticker.

Carle, Eric _____

Wells, Rosemary _____

Seuss, Dr. _____

Zolotow, Charlotte _____

Cleary, Beverly _____

Christopher, Matt _____

Kline, Suzy _____

Corbett, Scott _____

Andersen, Hans Christian _____

Brett, Jan _____

Choose two of these books to check out and read at home. Use them as part of your reading program.

You can earn two more stickers for this puzzle if you:

- Put the names of the authors in the correct alphabetical order.
- Put the titles of the books in the correct alphabetical order.

You can get a sticker for each book you read by one of these authors.

Where Can I Go?

When you find these words, cross them out with yellow crayon or pencil. One word goes in two directions. When you have located all of the words, you will have some letters left over. Circle them in red, and print them in the spaces below. Then connect the dots.

1 ● _____ **17**

Magazines	Homework	Computers	Programs	Me
Videos	Books	Cassettes	Kids	Where
Reading	School	Learn	Fun	You
Authors	Go	Oh	So	

2 ●   ● **16**

| M | C | O | M | P | U | T | E | R | S |
| A | A | A | L | R | G | O | I | E | C |

3 ●

G	S	U	H	O	M	E	W	A	H	● **15**
A	S	T	B	G	R	W	O	D	O
Z	E	H	A	R	R	H	R	I	O

4 ●

| I | T | O | Y | A | B | E | K | N | L | ● **14** |
| N | T | R | O | M | O | R | S | G | E |

5 ●

E	E	S	U	S	O	E	O	H	A	● **13**
S	S	F	U	N	K	I	D	S	R
V	I	D	E	O	S	M	E	Y	N

6 ●   ●   ●   ●   ●   ●   ● **12**

7   **8**   **9**   **10**   **11**

What Can I Watch?

Connect the dots. Color: G=Green, Y=Yellow, O=Orange, K=Pink, B=Blue, P=Purple. R=Gray.
Find one of these to check out and enjoy at home. Come back and tell us about it, and you'll receive
something special.

Title: _____

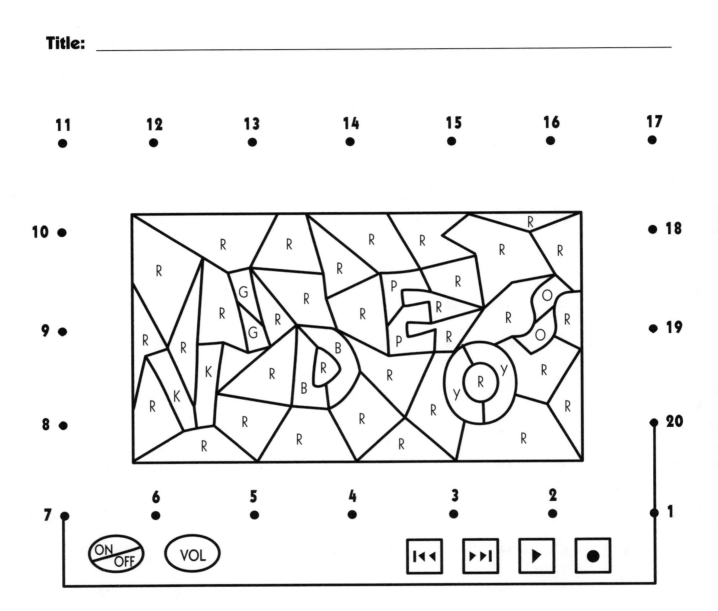

Number Please

Connect the dots. Match the Dewey Decimal numbers with the correct subject category. Print the underlined letters in the spaces to the right to spell out a secret message. Then, turn the paper over and complete the "Read to Learn" program on the back. Read some great books! When you are finished, bring this sheet back. There is a special surprise for you.

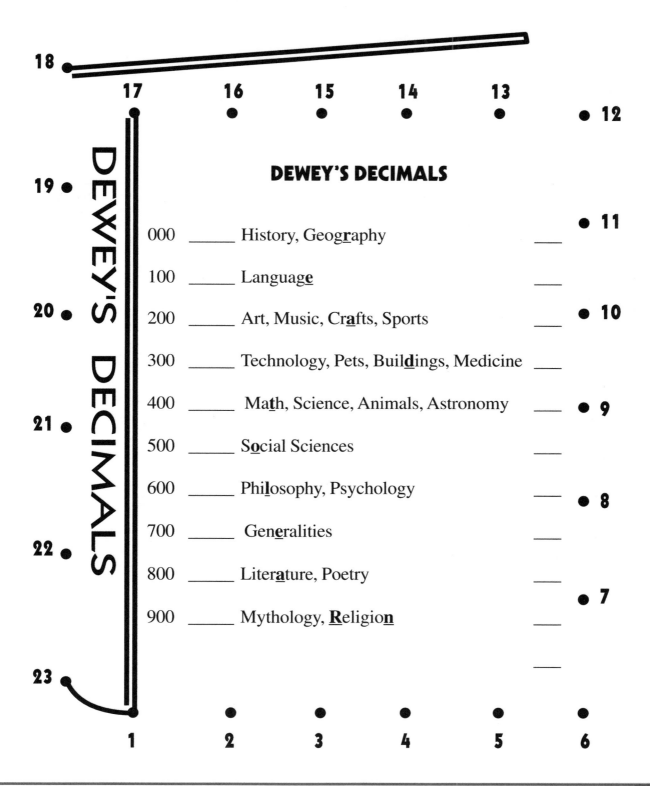

DEWEY'S DECIMALS

000 _____ History, Geog<u>r</u>aphy

100 _____ Languag<u>e</u>

200 _____ Art, Music, Cr<u>a</u>fts, Sports

300 _____ Technology, Pets, Buil<u>d</u>ings, Medicine

400 _____ Ma<u>t</u>h, Science, Animals, Astronomy

500 _____ S<u>o</u>cial Sciences

600 _____ Phi<u>l</u>osophy, Psychology

700 _____ Gen<u>e</u>ralities

800 _____ Liter<u>a</u>ture, Poetry

900 _____ Mythology, <u>R</u>eligio<u>n</u>

Read to Learn

Choose one book from each category. Print the title, author and call number in the spaces provided. Choose one of the following ways to report on each book. You must use each reporting method at least once, however you are free to choose which reporting method to use for each book.

    A. Draw an original picture that tells about something in the book.

    B. Write a paragraph that includes three interesting things you learned from this book.

    C. Write a paragraph telling how this book will help you.

    D. Make a diorama

    E. Make a time line.

    F. Give an oral report to your class or the librarian.

	Title	Author	Call No.
1. 000	_____ by	_____	_____
2. 100	_____ by	_____	_____
3. 200	_____ by	_____	_____
4. 300	_____ by	_____	_____
5. 400	_____ by	_____	_____
6. 600	_____ by	_____	_____
7. 700	_____ by	_____	_____
8. 800	_____ by	_____	_____
9. 900	_____ by	_____	_____
10. Biography	_____ by	_____	_____

Something Fun!

Down:

1. _____ usually come out once a month.

2. You can watch _____ on your TV.

3. It's fun to _____ !

Across:

1. You can listen to stories or music on audio _____.

2. You can _____ lots of interesting things at the library.

3. Sometimes we go to the library to _____ for a test.

It's fun to _____ _____ _____ _____ ! (Unscramble the circled letters.)

What Kind of Book Is This?

1. A person writes an ___ ___ ___ △ ___ ___ ___ ___ ___ ___ ___ ○ about their own life

2. A story that an author makes up is called ___ ___ ___ ☆ ___ ___ ___

3. Fiction books are filed alphabetically by the ___ ___ ___ ▢ ___ ___ ___ , ___ last name.

4. A ___ ___ ___ ___ ___ ___ ___ ___ ○ ___ ___ book gives us facts and information.

5. Nonfiction books are filed by Dewey Decimal ___ ___ △ ___ ___ ___ ___ .

6. A ○ ___ ☆ ___ ○ ___ ___ ___ ___ is a true book that an author writes about a real person.

7. We can look in the ___ ___ ___ ▢ ___ ___ ___ ___ ○ ___ to find the correct way to spell words.

8. We can find the ___ ▢ ___ ___ ___ ___ ___ ___ ___ ___ of a word using the dictionary.

9. If we want to find a true article about something, we can look in a book called an ___ ___ △ ___ ___ ___ ___ △ ___ ___ ___

10. An ___ ___ ○ ___ ___ is a book of maps.

11. We can find all sorts of fascinating facts in an ___ ___ ___ ___ ___ ○ ___ .

Fill in the spaces with the correct letters to get the secret message.

△ ___ ___ ___ ___ ☆ ___ ___ ▢ ___ ___ ___ ○ ___ ___ ___ ___ ___ ___ !

| **Hint:** Unscramble the letters! |

What Am I Supposed to Do?

Circle the first, third and fifth words. Underline the second, fourth and sixth words. Then do what the puzzles tells you to do. We'll give you something special when you come back to the library and tell us about it. Clue: Use a mirror!

Title: _____

Something Fun to Do

Unscramble these words. Print the circled letters in the spaces along the left side. Check one of these out. Use it in the library or at home. Come tell us about it, and we'll give you something special.

Title: _____

____	**KOOBS**	⊙ __ __ __ __
____	**DIVEOS**	__ __ __ ⊙ __
____	**TERSUCOMP**	__ ⊙ __ __ __ __ __ __
____	**TIKS**	⊙ __ __ __
____	**TYOS**	__ __ ⊙ __
____	**WARESOFT**	__ __ __ ⊙ __ __ __ __
____	**PACTCOM CSID**	__ __ __ __ __ __ __ ⊙ __ __ __ __
____	**SCHEATER**	⊙ __ __ __ __ __ __ __
____	**WORKHOME**	⊙ __ __ __ __ __ __ __
____	**SETTESSAC**	⊙ __ __ __ __ __ __ __ __
____	**ZINESMAGA**	__ ⊙ __ __ __ __ __ __ __
____	**MAGES**	__ __ __ ⊙ __
____	**ZUPZELS**	__ __ __ __ __ ⊙ __
____	**SAIDEPOLCYCNE**	__ __ __ __ __ __ __ __ __ ⊙ __ __ __
____	**TIONDICARIES**	__ __ __ ⊙ __ __ __ __ __ __ __ __
____	**LASTA**	__ ⊙ __ __ __
____	**MENTSASSIGN**	__ __ __ __ __ __ ⊙ __ __ __ __
____	**SYTDU**	⊙ __ __ __ __

Read One!

Connect the dots, and discover something fun that you can read. Color your picture.

Look in the Fairy Tale Section (398.2), and find one to read. Draw a picture of your favorite part of the story on the back of this paper. Bring it to us, and we will put it in our Fairy Tale Scrapbook for everyone to enjoy.

Title: _____

Grimm's Fairy Tales

Grimm's Fairy Tales

J 398.2 GRIMM

1 2 3 4 5 6 7 8 9 10 11 12 13 14 15 16 17 18

Try One, You'll Like It!

Circle the letter where the words meet. Unscramble the letters to decode the message. Find one, check it out and enjoy it at home. Come back and tell us about it. We have something special for you.

Title: _____

_____ _____ _____ _____ _____   _____ _____   _____ _____ _____ _____ _____!

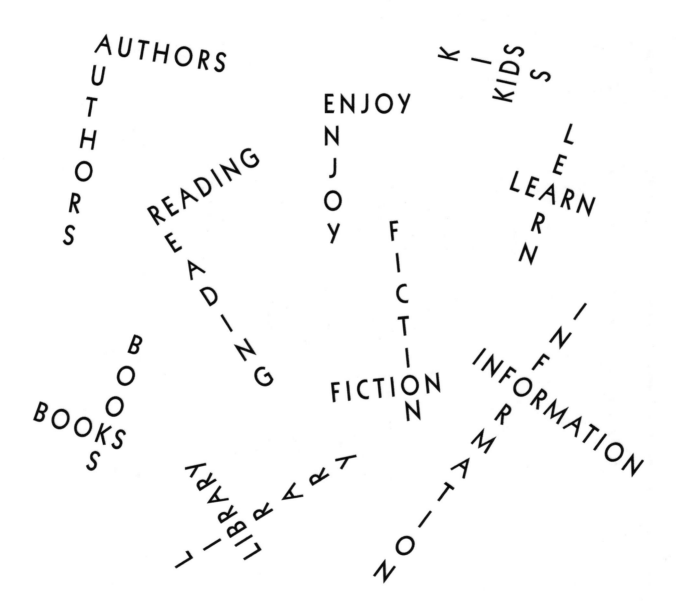

Fact Finding Fun

For questions 1–4 unscramble the words to complete each sentence. Then look in one of those kinds of books to answer the questions. For questions 5-7 decide which kind of book to use, and use it to answer the questions.

1. An **CLOENCPEDYIA** ___ ___ ___ ___ ___ ___ ___ ___ ___ ___ ___ ___ is filled with articles that give us information about things.

   Look up Abraham Lincoln. Remember we look up people by using their last name. Read the article and tell three facts about him.

   _____

   _____

   _____

2. An **STLAS** ___ ___ ___ ___ ___ is a book of maps. Look in one and locate these capitol cities. Bring the atlas to the children's reference desk, and show us.

   Springfield, IL_____   Concord, NH_____   Tallahassee, FL _____, Phoenix, AZ _____

3. A **TIONDICARY** ___ ___ ___ ___ ___ ___ ___ ___ ___ ___ gives us the proper spelling and definition of words. This book will also tell you the pronunciation, part of speech, and the number of syllables for each word. Look in one of these, and copy the word in syllables (include the accent mark), the pronunciation, the part of speech and the definition of each word,

   chase_____

   zither   _____

   jagged   _____

   quickly   _____

4. An **NACALM** ___ ___ ___ ___ ___ ___ ___ give us many interesting facts. Look in one and write down the answers.

   Three female gold medalists for women's gymnastics and the year they won.

   _____   _____   _____

   Three male gold medalists for men's ski jumping and the year they won.

   _____   _____   _____

5. Look in an _____ to find out where these national parks are located. Tell what year they were established.

   Yellowstone National Park   _____

   Everglades National Park   _____

   Acadia National Park   _____

   Yosemite National Park   _____

   Glacier National Park   _____

6. These words are spelled incorrectly. Look in a _____and print the correct spelling.

   acommodate _____   leeve _____

   sugjest _____   aple _____

7. Look in an _____ to see which states neighbor these states.

   Illinois _____   California _____

   Florida _____   Texas _____

You Are Special

Draw and color a picture of yourself having fun at the library. You can use this picture with the story you write on the back.

Your Name: _____

Grade: _____ **Age:** _____ **School:** _____

Fun at the Library

Write a story to go with your picture. Tell what you did at the library. If you need to, dictate your story to someone who can print it here for you. This story must be your own. It cannot be a story that you read in a book or heard somewhere else. It can be as long as you want it to be. You can even write a make believe story if you want to. Bring your story to the library, and show it to us. We will make a copy of it to put in our "Library Story Book."

_____

_____

_____

_____

_____

_____

_____

_____

_____

_____

_____

_____

_____

Your Name: _____

Grade: _____ **Age:** _____ **School:** _____

Songs and Poems

Write a poem about coming to the library. Draw a picture to go with it. Bring it to us. We'll copy it and put it into our "Library Story Book."

Choose one of these tunes and write a song about the library. "Jingle Bells," "Frere Jacques," "If You're Happy," "The Wheels on the Bus"

Your Name: _____

Grade: _____ **Age:** _____ **School:** _____

Storytime Fun

We want to go to Story Time at the library, but we can't find the Story Time Room. Can you help us?

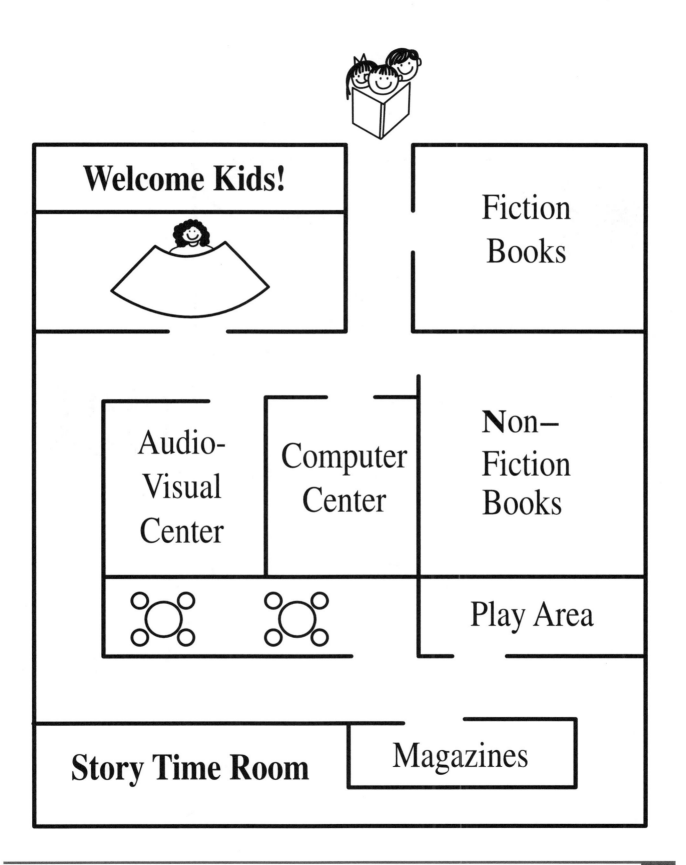

What Did You Say?

Decipher this puzzle and shout it out as loud as you can! Color P=Pink and R=Red. Then connect the dots.

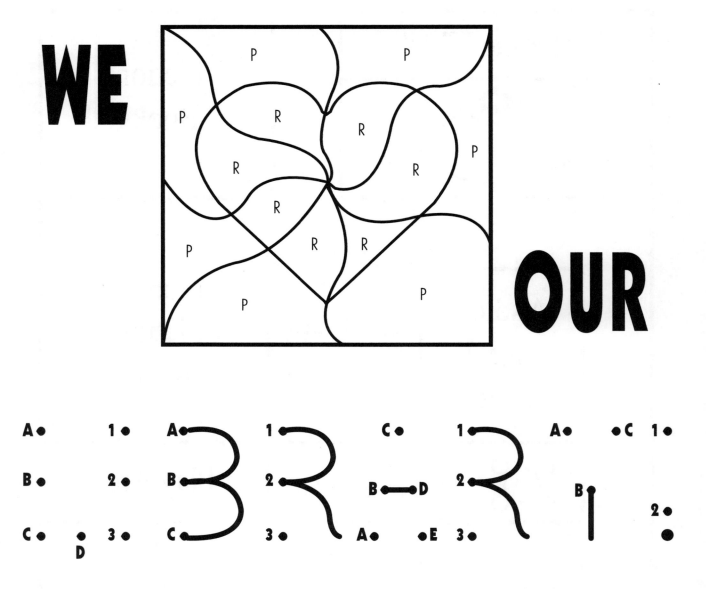

Library Fun

Fill in the letters to complete the following words. There will be a special message in the long, vertical box when you are finished.

Toys   Videos   Cassettes   Games

Learn   Read   Books   Videos

Encyclopedias   Homework   Programs   Youth

```
          O _ T H
          N C Y _ L O _ E D I A _
    C     S _ E T T E S
          O M _ W O R K


          E A _ N
    V     D E _ S
          O O K S
P R O G   A M S
    G     _ _ S
          _ _ _
    T O    S
```

Where Do You Want to Go?

Follow the letter path. Print the message in the space below.

_ _ _ _ , _ _ _ _ _ _ _ _ _ _ _ _ _ _ _ _ _ _

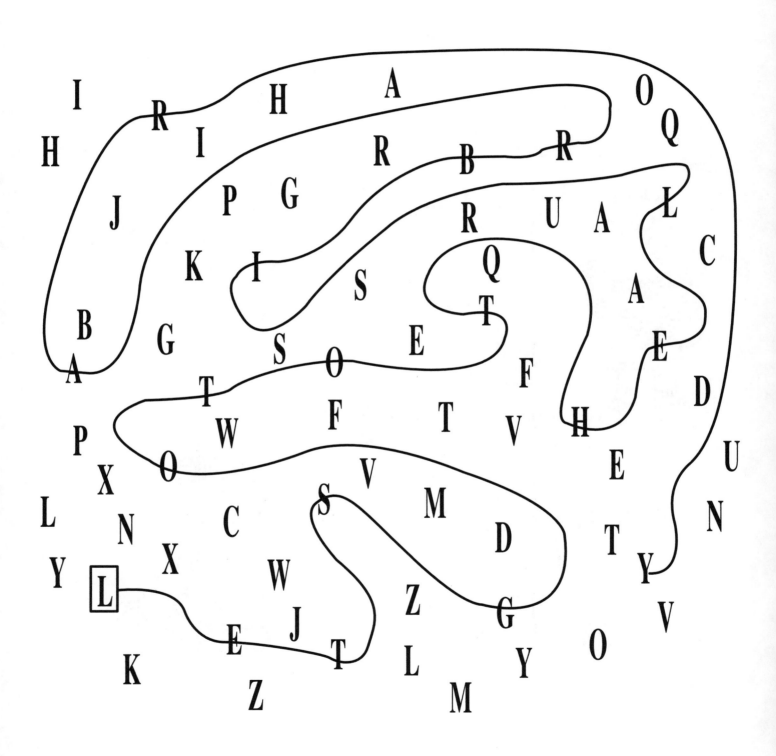

Shout It Out!

1=A   4=D   7=G   10=J   13=M   16=P   19=S   22=V   25=Y

2=B   5=E   8=H   11=K   14=N   17=Q   20=T   23=W   26=Z

3=C   6=F   9=I   12=L   15=O   18=R   21=U   24=X

___ ___ ___ ___ ___ ___ ___ ___ ___   ___ ___ ___
12 9 2 18 1 18 9 5 19   1 18 5

___ ___ ___ ___ ___ ___ ___   ___ ___ ___ ___ ___ ___ ___!
20 15 20 1 12 12 25   1 23 5 19 15 13 5

Using the same code as above, create your own library message for others to try.

Enjoy These

Fill in the missing letters to complete the following words. When you are finished there will be a message in the vertical box. Do what it says. Then turn over this page to find out what to do next.

Music Cassettes	Crafts	Humor	Cassettes
Biographies	Puzzles	Games	Books
Toys	Non-Fiction	Videos	Fairy Tales

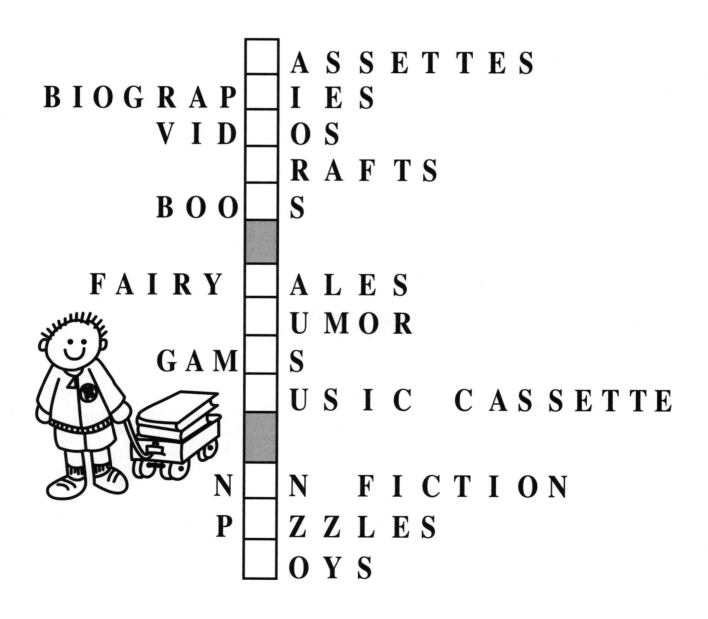

```
              □ A S S E T T E S
B I O G R A P □ I E S
        V I D □ O S
              □ R A F T S
    B O O □ S
              ▓
    F A I R Y □ A L E S
              □ U M O R
        G A M □ S
              □ U S I C   C A S S E T T E
              ▓
          N □ N   F I C T I O N
          P □ Z Z L E S
              □ O Y S
```

Enjoy These 2

Check out one of each of the things listed on the front out. Enjoy them at home. Print them in the spaces below. Then come back and tell us about them. If you complete this sheet, your name will be entered in a drawing to win a special surprise. You can choose any items you want in each category.

Story Cassette: _____
> (This can be a book/cassette packet or a book on tape.)

Nonfiction Book: _____

Toy: _____
> (You can play with a toy in the library and tell us about it. Be sure to put it back on
> the toy shelf when you are finished.)

Music Cassette: _____

Puzzle: _____
> (You can do a puzzle in the library. Show it to us when you put it together. Then, put it
> in the puzzle rack when you are finished.)

Game: _____
> (Try one of the games at our Library Game Table.)

Biography: _____

Video: _____

Crafts: _____
> (Make one of the crafts in the book you chose. Bring it in, and show it to us.)

Book: _____

Fairy Tale: _____

Humor: _____
> (This can be a funny story or a joke book.)

Puzzle Solutions

P. 57 **What's There?** Use Your Library

P. 59 **Read It!** Magazines

P. 60 **Fiction Fun** Sports, Animals, Mystery, Science Fiction, Humor, Family, Adventure, Fairy Tale, Folk Tale, School

P. 61 **Check It Out!** Cassettes

P. 63 **Where Can I Go?** Library

P. 64 **What Can I Watch?** Videos

P. 65 **Number Please** 900--History, Geography; 400--Language; 700--Art, Music, Crafts, Sports; 600--Technology, Pets, Buildings, Medicine; 500--Math, Science; 300--Social Sciences; 100--Philosophy, Psychology; 000--Generalities; 800--Literature, Poetry; 200--Mythology, Religion Read to Learn

P. 67 **Something Fun** Down 1. magazines, 2. videos, 3. books. Across 1. cassettes, 2. learn, 3. study. Read

P. 68 **What Kind of Book Is This?** 1. autobiography, 2. fiction, 3. author's, 4. nonfiction, 5. numbers 6. biography, 7. dictionary, 8. definition 9. encyclopedia, 10. atlas, 11. almanac. Come to the Library

P. 69 **What Am I Supposed to Do?** Books on tape. Check one out.

P. 70 **Something Fun to Do** books, videos, computers, kits, toys, software, compact disc, teachers, homework, cassettes, magazines, games, puzzles, encyclopedias, dictionaries, atlas, assignments, study. Books With Cassettes

P. 72 **Try One, You'll Like It!** Read a Book

P. 73 **Fact Finding Fun** 1. encyclopedia (He was 16th president, he abolished slavery, he was assassinated). 2. atlas. 3. dictionary (chās) verb--To follow rapidly; (zith´ r) noun--A musical instrument. It's a box with strings across it; (jag´ id) adjective A ragged, uneven edge; (kwik´ le) adverb--fast. 4. almanac--the answers will vary. 5. encyclopedia--Wyoming 1872, Florida 1934, Maine 1916, California 1890, Montana 1910. 6. Dictionary: accommodate, suggest, leave, apple. 7. atlas Illinois--Kentucky, Indiana, Missouri, Wisconsin, Iowa; Florida--Alabama, Georgia; California--Oregon, Nevada, Arizona: Texas--Louisiana; Arkansas, Oklahoma, New Mexico.

P. 78 **What Did You Say?** We love our library!

P. 79 **Library Fun** youth, encyclopedias, cassettes, homework learn, videos, books, programs, games, read, toys Yeah Library

P. 80 **Where Do You Want to Go?** We love our library!

P. 81 **Shout It Out!** Libraries are totally awesome!

P. 82 **Enjoy These** cassettes, biographies, videos, crafts, books, fairy tales, humor, games, music cassettes, nonfiction, puzzles, toys Check Them Out

Helpful Hints

- **Begin planning early.** Reserve program spaces and order special materials early.

- **Set up the program area prior to the program.** If you are doing treasure hunts, departmental visits, etc., make sure everything is in its place before the children arrive. Have all materials and supplies prepared ahead of time.

- **Be on hand to greet the children as they arrive.** Let them find their name tags and put them on. Take time to visit with them briefly before taking them into the program area.

- **Play recorded children's tapes while the children gather in the room.** This gives them something to do while waiting for the program to begin.

- **Make sure your assistants know what they are to do.** If you have people assisting you, meet with them a day or two prior to the program, so they are familiar with their responsibilities. For those helping with treasure hunts and departmental visits, make sure they know where to go and what to do.

- **If you need to shorten a program, try to keep the order of the program as is.** These programs have been carefully designed so they flow from one activity to another.

- **Avoid showing videos in place of sharing books.** Children need more "live entertainment." They need the interaction of a living, breathing person reading or telling a story rather than watching something on television. Remember that federal law prohibits the use of some videos in schools and libraries.

- **Try to offer each program more than one time.** Choose morning, afternoon, evening or weekend times. This allows you to accommodate more children and helps busy families attend library programs.

- **When doing these programs in schools, teachers and school librarians (resource center teachers) can work cooperatively to present them.** You can do one class at a time or combine several sections of each grade level. Learning Center teachers (school librarians) may spend a week doing each of these programs with different classes. When you do this, try to vary each program by using different stories, etc. Make adaptations as needed for various grade and ability levels.

- **Be sure to include special education students in your programs.** In public libraries it may be wise to include a child's parent in the program. In schools, work with special education teachers to develop an adapted program for those children who need it.

- **Check to see if children have food allergies or restrictions.** Be willing to substitute foods or have the child's parent bring a suitable snack.

Most of all, enjoy celebrating libraries. books and reading with children!

Publicity

Try some of these ideas to help advertise your program.

1. Include an article about your upcoming programs in the library or school newsletters and newspapers. Public libraries can request that schools include library programs in their newsletters. Be sure that this publicity is made available to them well in advance. Give information about the program date and time as well as registration information. Avoid announcing which stories will be shared during the program; let this be a surprise for your audience. Make your articles inviting, telling people that each program will include art activities, games, stories and snacks. See sample article on page 89.

2. Create large, colorful, eye-catching posters. Avoid having a "standard" poster design; these look so much alike, people tend not to notice them. Also avoid having too many posters in the same area at one time. Experiment with different shapes, sizes and colors. Some posters can be displayed vertically, others horizontally. Consider having an entryway poster that entices people to stop by the children's department to ask for information about a program. Each program includes suggestions for posters. Use these as a starting point.

3. Make individual flyers for each program, and display them with the posters in the children's department. Include all the program and registration information on your flyers.

4. Design an "Upcoming Events" flyer that can be distributed to children who visit the library with school classes or attend library programs.

5. Create a children's department program flyer that lists all the programs you are sponsoring for each season of the year. This can be issued quarterly.

6. Develop a mailing list from your patron files, and send each family or individual a monthly or quarterly newsletter that includes news about library programs. The U.S. Postal Service provides bulk rates, but you must get mailings to them early.

   An alternative is to invite patrons who desire to receive such mailings sign up to be on a mailing list.

7. If your library has a cable television or radio program, advertise programs there.

8. Make a large calendar that has 3" x 3" squares. At the beginning of each month, list daily events in each square. Include storytimes, school visits (both in house, and at schools) and special events programs. That allows patrons to see all that you offer.

9. When you assist patrons in the library, ask them if they are aware of the programs you have for children. Give them a flyer that lists all of your programming.

10. Let your friends and neighbors know about programs the library has for their children.

Sources

American Library Association
50 E. Huron St., Chicago, IL. 60611
(Information on libraries, books and reading, National Library Week, Caldecott and Newbery Awards)

Children's Book Council
568 Broadway Suite 404, New York, NY 10012
(Information on books, reading, Children's Book Week)

The following companies carry nametag patterns, party prizes, props, party decorations and more.

American Teaching Aids
4424 W. 78th St., Bloomington, MN 55435

Lakeshore Learning Materials
965 E. Dominiquez St., Carson, CA 90749

Bookmates
One Park Ave., Old Greenwich, CT 06870

Instructional Fair
P.O. Box 1650, Grand Rapids, MI 49501

Oriental Trading Company
P.O. Box 2308, Omaha, NE 68103

Party stores and teacher stores are also a good source of decorations, props, nametag patterns, etc.

Sample Article to Newspapers

You're Invited to a Birthday Party!

You're invited to celebrate _____ Library's birthday. Join us in the _____ Room as we gather to celebrate _____ years of library service to _____ *(town)*. Lots of fun awaits you as we tell amazing stories, read some cool books, play some awesome games and devour some delicious snacks! And we've been told to expect visits from some "surprise guests."

We will celebrate _____ Library's birthday from _____ to _____ *(time)* on ___ *(day)*, _____ *(month)* ____ *(date)*, ____ *(year)*. Children ages ____ through_____ are invited to register for this program beginning _____ *(date)*. You can register in person or by calling the Children's Department at _____ *(phone)*. This program is open to _____ Library cardholders only. You must present your _____ Library card when registering for this program.

We hope you can join us for this exciting celebration! If you have any questions, please call the Children's Department at _____ *(phone)*.

Hint

Keep a copy of all newspaper articles on file, so that you can refer to them if patrons have questions, comments or complaints.

Adapt this article for other programs in this book.

Sample Letter to Celebrities, Authors, and Teachers

Send on Library/School letterhead at least two months prior to your program.

Date

Dear _____:

We are preparing to celebrate _____ *(list event)* during _____ *(dates)*. To make our program special and enjoyable, the members of our staff are writing letters to famous American people (authors of children's books, teachers, principals etc.) asking them about their favorite books.

What were your favorite books as a child? Which authors did you like best? Do you remember your parents reading aloud to you or telling stories to you? If so, please share some of those memories with us. Did you ever receive books as gifts? If you have children of your own, we'd like to know what books you and your children enjoy (ed) sharing together. What are their favorites? Please tell us about memories of sharing stories with your own children.

If possible, we'd like you to send an autographed photo along with your letter. We will display your photo and letter during _____. At the close of our celebration, we will put your letter and photo into a scrapbook, so that we will always have these letters for children to enjoy while visiting the library. (For authors: We are going to create an Author's Alcove in the Children's Department where letters and photos of authors are on permanent display.)

We need to have your reply by _____ *(date)*. Thank you for helping us make _____ *(event)* special for the children of _____ *(city)*, _____ *(state)*. And thank you for helping children learn the value of reading. Happy reading to you!

Registration

Those of you presenting programs in public libraries might need to register the children who plan to attend. An index card system works well. Use 4" x 6" cards, and purchase a two-drawer file to accommodate them. These cards come in a variety of colors. They can be ordered through you paper supplier or local office products store.

Use a different color card for each session. Use dividers to separate each session. File each set of cards alphabetically by child's last name.

Use white cards for the waiting list. File them in a separate section in the order of registration. It helps to number these in the top right corner and note the date and time of registration. The first child on the waiting list will be the first invited if there is a cancellation.

The information on each card, allows you to gather interesting statistics. You can find out how many children from each school attend, the number of children from each age group/grade level and what areas of town the children are coming from.

It's recommended that you have printed copies of registration policies on hand. If people question your policies, you can present them verbally and in writing.

See the sample registration card below, and the waiting list card on the following page.

REGISTRATION CARD
(Please print neatly)

PROGRAM NAME: _____

DATE: _____ SESSION/TIME: _____

CHILD'S NAME: _____
(The way it is to appear on the nametag.)

CHILD'S BIRTHDATE: _____ GRADE: _____

CHILD'S ADDRESS: _____

CHILD'S PHONE: _____ SCHOOL: _____

CHILD'S LIBRARY CARD NO: _____

---

1. Use 4" x 6" index cards. Use a different color for each session.

2. File all the cards for one session together, alphabetically by last name.

3. Use dividers to separate each session in your file drawer.

4. If a child cancels, write the date of the cancellation on the card, and keep it in the back of the file. Note who called in the cancellation.

```
┌─────────────────────────────────────────────────────────────┐
│                    WAITING LIST CARD          Number _____ │
│                    (Please print neatly)                     │
│                                                              │
│   PROGRAM NAME: _____      │
│                                                              │
│   DATE: _____  SESSION/TIME: _____      │
│                                                              │
│   CHILD'S NAME: _____      │
│                                                              │
│   CHILD'S BIRTHDATE: _____  GRADE: _____      │
│                                                              │
│   CHILD'S ADDRESS: _____      │
│                                                              │
│   CHILD'S PHONE: _____  SCHOOL: _____      │
│                                                              │
│   CHILD'S LIBRARY CARD NO: _____      │
│                                                              │
└─────────────────────────────────────────────────────────────┘
```

1. Use 4" x 6" white index cards.

2. Number children as they register. Include date and time of registration.

3. File cards behind the waiting list divider in order of registration.

4. Move children from waiting list to a program in the order that they signed up.

5. When moving a child from the waiting list to a program, you can either fill out a color coded card or move the white card to the proper program slot. When you use the white card, note the session (time and day) the child moves to.

6. Save cards of children who cancel in a separate division titled, "Cancellations."

Room Set Up

This set up chart accommodates 30 children. Adapt it as needed for smaller or larger group. You may need to make further adaptations depending on the size and configuration of your area.

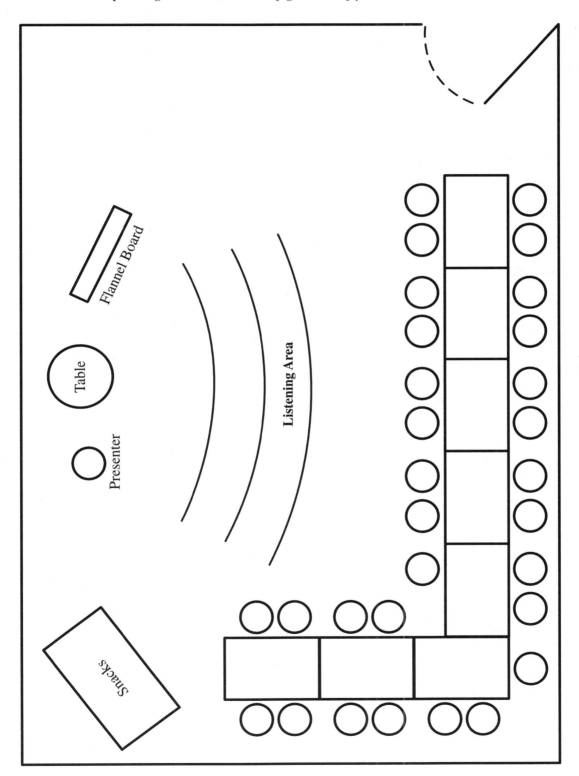

Flannel Board

Table

Presenter

Listening Area

Snacks

Activity Chart

	Birthday	Welcome	NLW	CBW	Dewey	Awards
Art	✔	✔	✔	✔	✔	✔
Author Visits			✔	✔		✔
Book Character Visits	✔	✔	✔			
Booktalks	✔	✔	✔	✔	✔	✔
Bulletin Boards				✔	✔	
Cheers	✔	✔	✔	✔		✔
Contests		✔				✔
Department Tours		✔	✔			
Games			✔	✔	✔	
Giveaways	✔	✔	✔	✔	✔	✔
Library Skills	✔	✔	✔		✔	
Music	✔	✔	✔	✔	✔	✔
Parent Programs		✔		✔		
Poetry				✔	✔	
Reading Programs	✔	✔	✔	✔	✔	✔
School Visits			✔		✔	
Service Projects	✔	✔	✔		✔	
Skits					✔	
Snacks	✔	✔	✔	✔	✔	✔
Special Guests	✔	✔	✔	✔	✔	✔
Story Sharing	✔	✔	✔	✔	✔	✔
Time Capsule	✔	✔				
Treasure Hunts	✔	✔			✔	

Note: To locate an activity, turn to the program list in the celebration you wish to use. Chapters begin on:

Index

Subjects are listed in CAPITAL LETTERS. Titles of activities, games and songs are listed in lower case letters. There is an Activity Chart on page 94.